# So You're Dead
## And Other Concerns of the Recently Deceased

Josh Stricklin

Copyright © 2023 Josh Stricklin

All rights reserved.

ISBN: 9798395031648

## DEDICATION
This book is dedicated to Garamond, the font.

Mamaw
I love you
Josh

This is a work of fiction.

Don't be foolish.

# ACKNOWLEDGMENTS

Hello. What you are holding in your hand, perhaps the words you are about to read would be more accurate, although it may seem like a book meant to help you in dealing with your own death, it is not a self-help book. If that wasn't clear to you, I hope I've reaching you before making a grave error. I certainly hope you didn't wait until then to read it. I assure you, it is fiction. This is also not a book for someone looking for YA Christian literature, perhaps for your troubled youth who had strayed from the path of righteousness. Don't worry, you wouldn't be the first to have been tricked by its mention of Heaven and Hell. Perhaps as an author I should be more straightforward with my themes. You will also not find any supernatural ghosts, or Voodoo demons, or shrieking sadist or green roses which have filled the pages of my other books. What you will find in this book is tongue-in-cheek attempt at being silly about a serious subject. My specialty. I hope when you purchased or rented this book, you understood that. Although if you manage to make it deeper than a few pages, I hope this book's actual themes speak to you. Or at least that you laugh.

XO

J

Don't forget to show compassion!

# Prologue
## AN ARTIST TAKES THE NUMBER NINE BUS

Black clouds hang over Lucas. The sky is a deep, hot orange. A swarm of locusts glides like an amoeba across the sky. He hears the roar of a demonic, world-destroying monster just beyond the skyscrapers. He feels it imposing on the city, lurking out of sight as if to rain down its unholy terror onto the streets. Lucas whimpers weakly and cowers on the sidewalk bench. "What are you people doing?" he demands of the ones who walk as far away from him as they can without stepping into traffic. "This is Armageddon! Rex! Rex, it will be OK!"

Someone speaks to him now, a soothing song piercing the cacophony in his mind. The voice is clearer than anything he has heard in years, and his full body flinches. "That's right, bud. It's going to be okay."

To Lucas's left, a skinny man stands wearing black jeans, a white button-up, Converse high-tops, and black sunglasses with circle lens and frames covering his eyes on the side like a blind person's. His deliberately messy, black hair falls over his forehead at random curves. The man's shirt sleeves are rolled up to the elbow, and the buttons are undone. Underneath it, Lucas sees the letters "UNDGAR" above a circular design on the chest. Lucas's face stretches open in fear of the man. He shrieks at the top of his lungs. He falls off the bench, knocking over a trashcan. The people on the sidewalk hurry away from him. He crawls away from the man, dragging himself through the fallen garbage.

"You're going to have to stop that," the man says. He extends his hand and leans over to Lucas. The man taps Lucas's left temple. A flash of not quite pain spreads down the side of his body. A pressure suddenly tightens and slowly releases, leaving his body hot and numb. "There we go."

Lucas's world brightens. Those flying things—the swarms of locusts, the dragons—dissolve into fluffy clouds. The layer of orange across his vision cools to a bright, clean blue. The buildings shine in the daylight. Lucas gasps at the world that has always been there.

The man says, "And that's what encephalitis does to the mind of someone who spent decades dropping acid."

The overwhelming sight of a world unsullied by infection or chemicals becomes normalcy in waves. Lucas turns to the man with wide eyes and short breath. "Are you Jesus?"

"Oh-ho-ho, no," the man says with a chuckle. "You can just call me Chris. No 'T,' just Chris."

"Are you Satan?" A prick of panic drilled into Lucas's heart.

"Come on. Do you think there are only two people in the afterlife?"

"Then who are you?"

"I'm a chauffeur."

"Where's your car?"

"Where I need to take you, we don't need a car."

Lucas's face scrunches up in confusion, and the idea that his mind was still muddy water reared its head. He wonders if this was just a new version of the world he had seen only moments before. "That's cryptic."

"Has to be."

"Why?"

Chris rubs his eyes. "Because you're going to die today."

A look of sheer panic flashes across Lucas's face. His eyes spring open. His lip trembles. An odd feeling of regret took up space within him.

"Look, it's no big deal," Chris says.

"You're the gr—"

"Grim Reaper?" Chris interjects. "That's a very offensive term. Come on, look at me." Chris removes his sunglasses, revealing a perfectly average-American face—clean shaven, free of any tattoos or piercings, maybe a little too boney, and a barely visible scar on his forehead but nothing horrible. His eyebrows raise as if to offer an unenthused *ta-da*. "Nothing *grim* at all. I keep it cryptic, so you won't assume exactly that."

"You're being mean about it."

"I'm sorry," Chris says. "They drill it in us to not let people think of us that way. Look, you're my only appointment today. Let's do something fun before we have to go."

"I'm the only person who's going to die today?" Lucas's eyes begin to water and the unfairness that this was only happening to him and no one else in the world causes his chin to quiver. He looks away from Chris.

"No, no, no," Chris dons his sunglasses. "There are over seven billion people on Earth. Even Heaven and Hell don't want anything to do with sorting things out. I work for a third-party company—Purgatory Enterprises—that handles it for them. We're not angels or demons. Just…people. In fact, someone's going to die in that building there in about sixteen minutes. My colleague, Aditi, will be handling that one, but I'll be with you. I'm here to make sure you know what to expect when it's over. Sort of an introduction to the orientation. Which brings me to my other purpose for being here today. What would you like to do before we head out? Make a wish. Within reason."

"I don't want to die."

"Oh, sure you do." Chris offers Lucas a hand and helps him to his feet. "It's pretty great honestly. You don't sleep anymore. That pain in your chest every time you sneeze? That's gone. No more people walking away in fear. No more hallucinations. No more waking up in random places you don't remember going."

"Is it the encephalitis?"

"What?"

"That kills me."

"Oh," Chris says, laughing, then suddenly stops. "No, no. No, it's pretty bad."

"What is it?"

"I can't tell you."

"Why not?"

"Because I want out of Purgatory. Even if it's too late to change it, if I tell you, they might put me somewhere I don't want to be. Come on." Chris leads Lucas to the bus stop at the corner. The number nine to Brooklyn hisses to a stop and the two get onboard. "So, what are we doing?"

Even with the infection at bay, Lucas cannot think of a single activity he recognizes as fun. He can't even think of a time when most of his day wasn't spent ducking out of the way of demons that weren't there. Lucas tries harder, digs deeper. There is no wife to see. No children to check in on. He looks out the window. Nothing even looks familiar to him. The buildings are gray, faceless skyscrapers. The people are strangers who move away from his smell as he finds a seat on the bus. He sees a kid walking next to his mother on the sidewalk. His chubby face and hands are glazed with melting chocolate ice cream from the cone he carries.

Nostalgia flashes through Lucas. It's the only memory that comes to him. When he was a kid, his dad took him to a Mets game. It was a hot afternoon, and there were only two things little Lucas wan-ted: a chocolate ice cream cone, and a foul ball. He only had to wait until the top of the second inning for the cone. During the seventh inning stretch, Lucas's dad told him that his mother tied herself to a tree branch and kicked the ladder out from under her feet. That was the last time chocolate ice cream tasted the same. The foul ball never came.

"I want to go to a Mets game," Lucas says. "And catch a foul ball."

"A painter wants to go to a baseball game? That's new, but I can do it," Chris says. His gusto distracts Lucas from the thoughts of his mother. Chris has a newspaper and peers into the columns. "I could, but the Mets don't play today. Well, they do, but they're in Chicago," Chris says, looking at his watch. "But, look! The Cyclones are playing. That's the Mets' minor league team. So…kind of the same. And we're already going to Brooklyn."

"Yeah," Lucas says, cheering up. "Yeah, let's do that."

Chris snatches the paper out of his face, stowing it under the seat. "Okay, let's do it." Chris's fingers fidget on his lap for a moment. He surveys the scenery around the bus. They aren't even close to the ballpark yet. "I guess we just wait for the bus to get there."

Usually, passengers make every effort to not make eye contact with anyone else while wobbling to the rhythm of the bus. Digging through purses. Using their cellphones. Looking at their hands. But not on this bus ride. Lucas is met with accusing glares, and up-turned noses.

"What's their problem?" Lucas asks. He looks down at his dirty hands. This isn't the first time he's regained consciousness covered in street filth.

"You think they recognize you from one for your art exhibitions or something?"

"They look mad."

"Oh. People just like to hate things. Probably not Soundgarden fans."

"What's Soundgarden?"

"What?" Chris nearly shouts and opens his white button-up to reveal a shirt that indeed says *SOUNDGARDEN* in bold red letters. "Are you even speaking English?"

Lucas shrugs and raises his eyebrows in a silent admission of guilt.

Chris drops the sides of the shirt. "Oh man. And you were alive in the nineties."

"Did a lot of drugs in the nineties."

"You must've been taking something surreal to miss out on—and please excuse the lack of hyperbole—the greatest band of all time."

"Are *you* even speaking English?" Lucas smiles. Chris playfully shoves him.

Lucas turns to the window. His smile falls away. The sun is bright and warms his cheek through the glass. He has forgotten what it's like to feel normal. To not see something horrible every time he opens his eyes. He watches the people on the street, not as real life, but as B-roll from a movie. "What's it like?" he asks Chris.

"Dying? You don't even feel it. Your adrenaline kicks in and you just kind of feel warm and numb. It's not as bad—"

"No," Lucas says. He watches the people on the sidewalk. "After that."

"Well," Chris says, pensive. He gestures to himself. "It's this."

"What does that mean?" Lucas lifts his head, leaving a smear on the window.

"There's a ton of paperwork. That takes...Hell, two months, I think—there's no clock in the room. You'll have questions about what's happening, and you can ask literally anything, so it's not totally boring. You'll learn the sins and what isn't a sin. Envy? No one cares. Envy is just fuel for change. Someone gets a new diamond-studded gimp suit, and you want one. Big deal. Happiness is key to this world. If you can find it, keep it. Blasphemy? No. Everyone has a sense of humor. That's what the paperwork says anyway. Lying? Suicide? Masturbation? No."

"What *is* a sin?"

"Murder. Rape."

"Sure," Lucas agrees, shrugging his shoulders.

"Passing in the turning lane."

"What?" Lucas turns his full attention to Chris.

"Not using a blinker when people are waiting on you."

"Are you serious?"

"Oh, yes," Chris states. "Most of the sins only took up a page or two. A bunch of 'don't be a dick'-type rules. But then mankind invented automobiles. Filled up a book. Then mankind invented airplanes, and they had to start over."

"Why planes?"

"Being in the heart of New York City, I don't think it's much of a stretch to come up with one big sin. Although if you don't remember Soundgarden, I can't imagine the World Trade Center was even a blip on your radar. But people treat the attendants like sub-humans. There are the seatbacks, the cramped spaces, getting up when you're not supposed to. Not to mention, there are so many people who don't know proper armrest etiquette."

"Oh," Lucas says. "So really just...be considerate?"

"That's basically what every religion says to do."

Lucas agrees. "Then where does your job come into play?"

"Well, once you finish your paperwork, then you work at Purgatory Enterprises."

"As grim reapers?"

"Chauffeurs," Chris corrects. "Yeah."

"But what's the point if you don't go to Heaven or Hell?"

"We do. Well, that's what they're called now. Originally it was Celestia and Bossier City, but about fifteen hundred years ago people wouldn't stop calling it Heaven and Hell. So, they changed it. But basically, each person I escort to the next place gives their feedback on how well I do. If I get three tens in a row, boom. I go to heaven. If I get three low scores in a row, I go down in the elevator. It's just being compassionate about what another soul is going through. They think people have forgotten how to do that."

"Wait, you're telling me your soul's damnation teeters on how well you perform on a scale of one to ten?"

"Well, ten's the highest score you can get," Chris says. "One's not the lowest anymore. More choices caused more variations in numbers. It got to where more people were working at Purgatory than were dying. They shortened the scale. More people were willing to give up the ones they had acquired than the people who had tens—mainly because they're easier to get—so they cut it in half, moved it to a six to ten scale. Cleared things up quick."

"That's weird," Lucas says.

"Eh, it works." Chris says. "They're not that different, you know—Heaven and Hell. The football teams are evenly matched. Both have AC units in all the houses."

"Then who cares where you go?"

"Because 'death do us part' only applies if you want it to. My wife is in Heaven."

"How do you know?" Lucas can see the stadium slowly approaching.

"She's a dog person," Chris says.

"So?"

"All dogs go to heaven, Lucas." Chris says, plainly. Lucas stares at him, dumbfounded. "They made a movie about it."

"That can't be true."

"It is," Chris says, stone sober.

"The only difference between Heaven and Hell is the pets?"

"Well, pot is better in hell. Plus, it's darker at night and graffitied in neon colors everywhere like a 90s anti-drug commercial. I guess they're not *exactly* the same. You'll get into all that later."

Lucas lays his head against the window. He watches with the overwhelming clarity of a world, unfiltered. He can't remember the last time it looked this way. When he thinks back on the last few decades, he can't remember much at all, but one thing comes to mind as vivid as the view from the bus seat.

He remembers being nervous at first. It was opening night at his first exhibition in '81. He was surrounded by twenty or twenty-five of his best pieces in a room with about as many people. His childhood friends came and left with words of praise, one of them even took home a small canvas painting of a cloaked man on a black throne titled "The Crimson King." It was the cheapest thing in the building, and Lucas appreciated the gesture. His dad and stepmother left with the first painting in the "Blueleaf Tree Forest" series.

He hugged his dad and kissed his stepmother—who graduated high school a year or two before he did—on the cheek. When they left, he noticed two men dressed in form-fitting suits, with deep V-neck tee shirts in pastel colors. They approached him, holding empty champagne glasses. They were impressed and just *had* to meet the artist, the one with the black duck's ass haircut told him. The one with the bright yellow spiked hair said nothing. They bought three of his most expensive paintings with cash. Sure, you could sell to your friends, or your family, but these two, they only knew him as an artist. Lucas's hands trembled with excitement as he thanked them. He offered to bring the paintings to their car, but they declined saying the three they wanted wouldn't fit. They would send someone for them. They offered something else though.

The bleach-blonde offered a sandwich bag of powder.

*Do a bump?* the one with the black hair said. He reached into the bag and brought out a small clump of the powder pinched between his fingers. He sharply snorted it into his nose. *It's a celebration!* he shouted. Lucas apprehensively stuck his fingers into the bag.

That moment stayed with him, buried in a pit in his mind beneath burnt spoons, orgies, and the taste of cinnamon. There's not much after that. What remains of his past fades into the rumbling view through the bus window. That feeling of his first sell rushes back into him, making his hands tremble. He becomes aware of the life he missed by taking every drug in the world to escape it. "I don't want to die," he whispers. His shaky fingers touch his left temple.

"You alright?"

"I'm fine. Just aches. Apparently, I have encephalitis."

"It'll pass," Chris assures him. Then he sees the ballpark's marquee inch into view. He motions for Lucas to pull the cable to stop the bus. "Come on," Chris's voice beckons Lucas out of the seat.

Lucas sees the ballpark, and excitement races through him.

The marquee welcomes the world to MCU Park with big blue letters. It draws Lucas's eyes up and up to the bright clean sky. The sun warms his face. He feels the electric atmosphere of baseball gameday. The smells of grilled burgers and hotdogs tickle his nose with a vibrancy that he could only recall from his childhood. The sound of an organ playing echoes into the parking lot. Children laugh as they pass. The world around him is different. The greens are greener, and the pinks are pinker. Even the blues and yellows and reds of the team logo shine like fireworks across his vision. His hand makes subtle swiping gestures at his side as though he is painting what he was seeing. No one shies away from him. No one even looks at him for more than a glance.

"Hey, bud," Chris says. "You get your ticket? It's only three bucks."

Lucas turns to him like a man coming out of sleep. "Huh?"

"Apparently the Mets on TV are more interesting than the Cyclones at the park. Don't get the one for two-fifty in the grass. Trust me. We're going for foul balls."

Lucas rummages through his pants and coat, dropping pocket debris around his feet, and finds a clip of brand-new singles folded in half. He pulls away three ones and absentmindedly hands them to Chris.

"I would hand that to them," Chris says. He gestures toward the box office. "General admission, and we'll sit by the foul pole."

Lucas waits for the two people ahead of him to finish and slides his bills under the cutout of the window. The breeze of the air conditioner rushes over his dirty hands like water. "It's cool in there." He laughs weakly.

The young woman on the other side takes the small stack of papers and smiles. He's too distracted by the cool air to notice the repulsion there. "Grass or general admission?"

"General admission," he answers.

He picks up the ticket, leaving a smear everywhere his fingers touch.

"Come on," Chris says. He jogs up to the ticket taker and drops his ticket in the little basket at the podium rather than handing it to the old man with the whizzbang mustache, and bright blue Cyclones jersey. The ticket taker doesn't notice. Chris walks through the metal detector spinning like a ballerina.

Lucas follows him. He hands the ticket to the mustachioed man and notices the grimace twisting the man's mustache up on one side. Lucas smells himself before realizing he's doing it. His cheeks flush, and he frowns. "I—"

"Nah, fuck that guy," Chris calls back. "He tears paper for a living. He's nobody."

Lucas takes his half of the ticket and walks through the silent metal detector. That ache in his head swells again, bringing a sharp pain in his ribs with it. Lucas folds in half coughing and groaning in pain.

Chris scrambles over to him. "Whoa, you got this, bud. Just breathe through it. It's all part of the process. Let's try straightening up. People are acting weird about it."

Lucas straightens, holding his ribs. His labored breathing makes him look like a sprinter with a stitch in his side. He groans. Chris breaths heavily, waving his hands to cultivate a rhythm. Without realizing it, Lucas matches his breathing, and the fire shooting down his left side withers to a smoldering numbness.

Lucas straightens, red faced and breathing heavily as if he had just been choking. "I thought you were tapping out early. Don't leave me here by myself. You're the only person that can give me directions. Let's get you a soda. You still have some cash, right?"

Lucas wipes his eyes. "Yeah. I thought that was it."

"Don't you worry. What's your drink? They only have Pepsi stuff. That sucks."

"Pepsi's fine."

"Oh, good."

When Lucas reaches the front of the concession line, the pain in his ribs is a memory. He has enough cash for a Pepsi and a hotdog. He hands the remainder of his money to the woman and receives no change.

*If this is my last meal, I might as well go all out.*

"Hot dog!" Chris says when Lucas turns to him. "I'm kind of hungry myself."

"You still get hungry?"

"You never stop getting hungry," Chris says. He points Lucas in the direction of the bleacher seats behind right field. "Stadium's empty. We might be the only people over there."

Across the field is the skyline of an amusement park. Lucas hears the spirited screams of people on the rollercoaster and almost second guesses his decision to come here. Then that familiar organ progression plays through the speakers. It winds faster and faster until—

*da-da da dah da-daahhh*
The smattering of fans shout "Charge!"

For a moment Lucas stands, watching the crowd. There is a glimmer of childlike wonderment in his eyes as the pitcher throws out the opening pitch.

"Lucas!" Chris calls. "I found the perfect seats."

Lucas hops up the bleachers. "I can't believe I'm here. The players are so close."

"You might want this," Chris says, tilting his head to the worn leather glove sitting between them on the metal bleacher seat.

Lucas finishes his hotdog in a couple bites and takes the glove. When he slides it on, it fits like a mold of his hand. He pounds his fist where the ball will land the way everyone who has ever worn a glove has done. The crack sound of baseball on wood snares Lucas's attention, drawing his sight to home plate.

The ball flies through the infield between shortstop and second base and bounces just before the centerfielder can get his hands on it.

Lucas deflates back onto the bleacher.

"Don't worry, bud," Chris says, leaning back on the bench behind him with his arms splayed to each side. "Got eight and a half more innings to go. We'll get it."

Lucas takes a sip of his soda. It wasn't a Coke, but it was ice cold. More ice than soda. Perfect. Most people growing up said that a glass bottle was the best way to drink a soda, but Lucas never cared what it was in as long as it was ice cold. So cold that only a few sips on a hot day would turn his chest to ice.

He remembers those days on the beach with his mom. Learning how to be responsible. He had taken the two quarters from his mom across the sandy beach, wobbly, but not too bad. Mom always took him to the beach on those nights where she and Dad had been too busy, and forgot to tuck him in. He had gotten the hang of the walking thing, but that sand unlocked a new level of difficulty. Lucas took the quarters to the man behind the stand right where the beach met the wooden boardwalk. The stand was a rolling cooler decorated with faux bamboo and a red and white beach umbrella. Lucas asked for a Coke, sliding the two circles across the wet surface of the cooler.

"Can I have a lot of ices?"

The man behind the stand smirked. His mustache crooked up to one eye, which he winked. He filled the paper cup to the top with ice, and poured a full can over it. The tiny bubbles sizzled in the heat of the day. "There you go, kiddo," he said, dropping a straw into the drink. "Tell your mom, pretty ladies drink for free."

"Okay!" Lucas said, grabbing the cup with both hands. He took two big, excited gulps and felt the air in his chest chill.

He crossed the sandy beach back to the towel and umbrella where his mother waited, a bright grin beneath her oversized, plastic sunglasses. She always wore those glasses the days after she forgot to tuck him in. Once even when it rained. It had gotten to the point when Lucas tucked himself in that his imagination took over his thoughts, trying to guess what fun adventures he and Mom would go on the next day. He notices a strange dark color peeking around the rim of the sunglasses. This had always stuck with him. He stared at it for a moment, remembering how he felt as perception and reality wrested in him, not in his mind, but in his heart, where he felt it the most. That color had always just been stray eye shadow, but now with time on his side, the experience of seeing her wince as she applied more and more makeup to her face, to that eye. Had he heard them those nights he went to sleep all—

"Did you give the man your quarters?"

"I did!" Lucas said, as he sucked down more of the tingly, fizzy soda and smiled.

"Great job, Luey," Mom tousled his hair. "You want to go swim?"

"Yeah," Luey said at a near screech. He took another big gulp from the cup and handed it to Mom. His feet padded toward the water, sending small splashes of sand up behind him. He giggled as Mom called to him, telling him not to go too deep. And he didn't. He stayed bouncing in knee-high water. Water splashed around him as he giggles and tries to get Mom wet. Then he feels something. A tingle at first. Then piercing, electric pain wrapped around his leg.

Luey shrieked.

Mom bolted up from the towel, sprinting to Luey. She pulled him out of the water, and he felt something fall away, releasing him. When he looked down he saw red lines covering one leg. The pain was incredible. His body jostles in her arms as she carries him back to the towel. He feels his mother set him on the ground, but it's not sand beneath him. It's something hard and cool. She hands him his soda. He hears her telling him that it's okay. Everything's okay. There's a calmness to her voice, but sobs threaten. He holds the soda with both hands and lifts his face to the sky.

Lucas can feel the warmth of the sun on his face. The waves solidify, losing the ebb and flow, smoothing back into the low roar of the baseball stadium again. His mother's soothing voice becomes masculine, and Lucas remembers that a man named Chris took him to a baseball game. He remembers that this is the last thing he'll get to do.

It's somewhere in the middle of a conversation about what it would've been like to be Chris Cornell's chauffeur when the voice through the speaker announces, "Bottom of the fifth. One out. Next at bat, shortstop, number—"

Chris bolts upright. "Look alive. I got a good feeling."

Lucas perks up, smacking his fist in the glove. The sky had just started to darken, turning the clouds a pink cotton candy color against a blue background. The hecklers in the crowd have mostly gone silent since the score evened out at two, so when the first pitch hit the catcher's mitt, Lucas heard it pop from his seat all the way across the park.

"Just a ball," Chris says.

The second pitch flies to the plate, and this time the batter swings. The crack of the bat echoes across the park. The ball storms toward a light pole like a beam.

Chris taps Lucas on the arm, "Here it comes! Here it comes!"

The ball bangs off the pole, slowing it just enough for Lucas to get underneath it. The ball falls delicately into the glove just as a few kids from nearby seats close in on him. Lucas closes his grip around the ball, sending the kids' back to their seats with unfulfilled expectations.

Lucas turns the glove over, not fully believing what he had done. He stares down at it, mystified. A low rumble of applause surrounds him. He looks across the park to the big screen and sees himself. He raises his glove, and the crowd cheers. It's not a deafening roar, but it's for him. The screen cuts back to the pitcher.

"You did it!" Chris screams, throwing his fists over his head.

"I did it," Lucas repeats. He drops back down in his seat. He warms with the heat of stage fright. There's a second moment when he feels like he is the only person in the world this is happening to. He smiles.

Then a sharp sting crawls down his body. It is a burning pain that doubles him over. He drops the ball and grabs his ribs, drawing everyone's attention.

"Oh no," Chris says. "Come on, let's walk this off."

Lucas focuses his weight on the bleacher, deciding between leaving and doing the only thing left to do, or writhing in pain in front of all these people who were suddenly looking at him *that* way again.

"You don't want this to be the last thing you see." Chris says.

Lucas reluctantly stands from the bleachers and eases back down the metallic steps. This time "walking it off" doesn't abate the pain. He crosses the walkway, past the concession stands. Lucas tries to run. "It hurts."

Chris doesn't try to slow Lucas. "I know. It's going to at first."

"I can't do this. I don't want to die."

"That's not how this works," Chris says a few feet behind him. He could easily catch up, but that never crosses Lucas's mind.

"Get away from me," Lucas shouts, attracting more attention.

"Come on," Chris says. "We were doing so well."

The light at the corner turns green just as Lucas charges past the man with the mustache. He's in the middle of the block. The number nine bus moves. The driver isn't flooring the pedal, but the bus only needs half a block to become fatal.

"I need a doctor!" Lucas shouts as the sky burns orange again. He freezes in place staring into the sky his broken brain presents. The things in the sky are flying toward him.

"Hey, calm down, bud."

Lucas turns to Chris. "Get away from me!" As Lucas turns away, Chris's face wrinkles up like someone bracing for a jump scare in a horror movie.

Lucas watches for cars coming from the right, but not for buses coming from the left.

Everything is black.

Then Lucas opens his eyes. He sees the world as if on its side. People are frantically scrambling across his vision, their faces horrified and open. He doesn't hear anything at all but a single pair of footsteps, and it isn't until he tries to move that he realizes he can't.

"Hey, bud," Chris says with sympathy. He kneels in the view of Lucas's far-off gaze. Lucas tries to move, even manages to utter one final groan. "No, don't try to fight it. You'll make it hurt." Chris takes a deep breath. "So, this is the point where the flash before your eyes catches up to reality. It's not so bad, right? Just a burn and some numbness. I really am sorry. I know that wasn't a good show, but you didn't have much to pull from. Your dad was kind of a schmuck, and your mom wasn't around. You were always a darker shade than everyone you knew. I tried to stop the side eyes, but sometimes the things you see every day won't change no matter what you do. But, hey! I got your ball.

"You're going to fit in here. You'll get your mind back, and you can paint again. Hell, maybe dying will give you some inspiration. You should see your legs. It's *real* gross. Hey, do you know where Lexington is? Kidding. I'm looking forward to working with you. Unless I get some more tens—wink and elbow. The EMTs are coming, so let's get out of here."

# Part 1
# Purgatory Enterprises

# Chapter 0
## A POINT OF NO RETURN

Death is a funny thing. It's the quintessential that'll-never-happen-to-me event that happens to all of us. So why not make it fun? That's Chris Anderson's theory on the matter. But death wasn't on his mind when it happened to him—even though it came rushing up to him on a gravel back road decades too early—it's rarely on anyone's mind at that age. And as he crossed that point of no return, he saw the best moments of his life flash before his eyes, as everyone does. Head jerked back on his shoulders, he fell to the ground, but in that moment, he saw her.

She pulled him through the crowd, her hair, a short auburn ponytail, bounced behind her all the way to the front barricade between the crowd and the stage. He remembered being lost in lyrics that sounded like the ramblings of someone in a fever dream. Something about purple toupees and the president's ear wax set to upbeat music from a jumping indie band playing their quirky hearts out. He also remembered feeling happier than he had ever been in his life. Andrea could've invited her roommate or anyone else in the world who actually knew the band's name, something that had still eluded Chris, but she had invited him, her boyfriend of only a couple weeks, into her world. She hopped, arms raised, to the rhythm of the music. He heard her voice over all the others. The crowd behind nudged him closer to her. He pressed against her, expecting resistance, a push back or a lean forward, but he was surprised when her hand lowered and hugged his face to hers. They stood cheek to cheek, burying the moment deep in his heart. He remembered kissing her next, but that didn't happen. Instead, he felt himself falling backward. He jerked as if from a falling dream. Chris's chauffeur, and older midwestern man named Henry, lead him to the next vision, taking him toward the next moment, nudging him closer with each word.

Chris sat at the dining room table; two printed job offers lay before him.

"I hardly think you should be making a big deal about this," Andrea said. He could feel her standing there, her body against his, her presence filling the room like sunlight. Her weight leaning against his back. Her hands slid down the front of his shirt, coming together in a loose hug. "Either one will be great for you."

"One's further away, but it pays a little more."

"And the other one has better benefits."

"They have the same benefits," Chris said.

"Well, with this one," Andrea said, pulling the job offer that would be nearby toward the two of them. She kissed him between the jaw and ear. Chris's heart leapt at the smell of her shampoo. "You'll be home sooner."

The decision was made.

This comes to him because it was the moment that Andrea and he became more than just a couple, but partners in everything they did. Chris came to the table with a decision to make, and Andrea would help come to a conclusion. It continued that way until she was no longer there to help. And after that he sort of floated through everything Henry had to show him, his first touchdown in the peewee league, getting a puppy and his best friend through grade school, even his parents finally getting married when he was ten years old, all with that lingering sweet shampoo aroma following him through his past.

He watched his life play before him as Henry, a rather charming and kind chauffeur himself, distracted from the jarring, falling sensation his body felt. But eventually Chris would hit the ground and lie in the grass, eyes up to the sky where he would inevitably be found.

Death isn't just funny. In that same funny way we all try to avoid it, death is always traumatic. The most traumatic thing many people will do. Which is why a therapist is the first person we meet on the other side. That, and the next life isn't always what we expect.

Before you see your loved ones, before you go through orientation, before you've even had your next meal, you speak to a calming voice to explain what has happened and what will happen. Because you don't bring anything with you from life to life, nothing physical anyway, but death can give you something that stays with you that even the next life can't get rid of.

You don't forget a thing like dying. Most people carry it with them at every stage of the next life. It won't be obvious, but if you're looking, you can see it. They wear it on their faces when they think no one is looking. It silences them for moments at a time during the day. May even be the reason they cancel plans or avoid taking the bus. Rest assured, death changes you. And the one thing that doesn't change about it, whether you go in a hospital bed, or crash into the side of a mountain with three hundred other passengers, you will have to do it alone. Much like your time at Purgatory Enterprises, it is an experience uniquely yours. So, enjoy it the best you can.

# Chapter 1
## I'M ON THE CHOPPING BLOCK, BABY!

Chris remembers dying even all this time later. The bright blue sky and overgrown grass surrounding his vision. The white-hot numbness in his head. The way he disconnected from his body, piece by piece. The way it felt like he was the only person in the world this was happening to. He thinks about this every time he waits to dial in the combination to his mailbox in the bright, cream-and-brass-colored halls of the Purgatory Enterprises mail office. Today, the halls are alive. The chaotic energy surrounding Chris is like a current of electricity he's trying to avoid. Something about being murdered changed him. He is uneasy around people he doesn't know. He keeps his distance, standing against the wall like a nervous teenager. People run up and down the halls with tears of joy in their eyes. Others slam the mailboxes shut, the sound reverberating through the walls.

Chris sees a woman punching a hole in the wall by the exit as he tries to look anywhere but in that direction. In the opposite corner, a swirling mass of limbs spins into existence as the two guys from the Hell side of purgatory celebrate a second consecutive low score. People are running down every corridor at full speed, screaming, laughing, singing, fighting. A guy with long dreadlocks wearing a bright tie-dyed tank top and purple shorts jumps up and slaps the sign indicating the range of mailbox numbers down the adjacent hallway. Most people can just follow their instincts to their mailbox. Something in the essence of a person knows how to get where they're going on the campus of Purgatory Enterprises, so most people don't need the signs. However, even though the essence of a person knows how to navigate the campus, and people can follow their instincts much easier after death, people still need the signs. Chris inwardly groans at the frat house vibe of the building to which he is still not adjusted. And to make things worse, over the speakers, a Prince song is egging them on, telling his listeners to go crazy, to get nuts even.

At the end of the hallway there is an elevator waiting behind a golden door with a keycard entrance, and only two destinations: Heaven or Hell.

Chris waits across the width of the corridor as the person with the mailbox above his, who is soaking wet and wearing nothing but a towel and necklace, dials in the combination. The man, with his wet, slicked back hair, bends forward to see the dial better. The towel threatens to loosen, springing free everything beneath it. Chris averts his eyes to one of the myriad navy and ocher posters reminding everyone of the rules to the Purgatory Enterprises.

The 8 Areas of Review
(as established by the Guild of Divinity)
The average of each section rounded to the nearest
whole number creates your overall score:

1. Compassion
2. Knowledge
3. Sincerity
4. Helpfulness
5. Connection
6. Pain
7. Compassion
8. Overall

<u>Remember to show *Compassion*!</u>

Chris has read this so many times that he doesn't register the words anymore, he only remembers the information all at once. He can almost feel the ruts that his eyes have made over the months of tracing the same lines over and over, like a worn path. He shifts to the fine print at the bottom of the poster.

*\*3 consecutive high scores allow access to Heaven,*
*\*3 consecutive low scores allow access to Hell*

The guy in the towel wiggles once more and the door to the

mailbox springs open. He rips the envelope in half and finds the last page, the one with the results of his survey. An exhausted exhale of relief pours out of him, and he whoops with excitement. "Six point four," he announces. The gilded Star of David dangled onto his muscular chest. "Almost a seven."

"Yeah," Chris says, not really knowing what else to say. This is a common occurrence ever since Chris commented on the pendant of the necklace that matched the one branded on one of the many leather bracelets on Chris's wrist. It's the only thing he ever wears that isn't a towel as far as Chris has seen, so naturally it was the only thing he could find to make small talk about. Then the two were waiting for the person below Chris's mailbox to finish. "Way to go."

"Yeah, mofo!" The guy struts toward the Hell side exit, his feet slapping on the floor like a fish. Chris steps in the puddle of water in front of his mailbox. A few feet away a couple fall against the wall, seemingly trying to lick the molars out of one another's mouths. Chris cringes away from them.

Finally, Chris gets the mailbox open. He swipes the two pieces of mail and carefully makes his way through the hysteria to the Heaven-side exit. The heavy double doors to the mail office boom closed, trapping the chaos inside. Chris shoves the postcard sized memo from the Guild under his arm—those postcards rarely discuss anything regarding Chris—and opens the envelope with his latest score. He sees Lucas's name, and skips over the questionnaire answers straight to the scores on the back of the third page. At the bottom, above Lucas's signature reads:

Average Section Rank: **9.9**
Official Final Score: **10**

Chris grips the paper and pumps his fist one, two, three times. He looks around for anyone watching. More people are pumping their fists, so he pumps one last time, dropping the postcard. He picks the card up and turns it over until the words are legible. The postcard is a fiery red. The black words on it reflect light like glass. The mailbox room is a typical method for massive dissemination of information. People check their mailboxes every day, hoping against hope for an early feedback score. The Guild sends regular amendments to Purgatory Enterprises protocol. Rule updates, member housing reassignments, or in this case, new perks for the recently deceased:

Consummate Professional,

The Guild of Divinity has agreed to offer a new chance for the recently fallen to be greeted by loved ones in an effort to ease the transition from one life to the next. This is only a test run and may only be a perk for a limited time. But after thousands of research hours, and numerous surveys, we believe this will create a much more positive experience for Purgatory Enterprises employees. For the near future, all volunteers may register with the Office of Orientation. For more information, leave all queries in your mailbox.

Best,

The Guild of Divinity.

*So, does this mean we can see one of* our *loved ones who have died?* Chris wonders.

All along the sidewalk, there are street performers, which brings Chris's thoughts to the business of choosing what he wants to do forever. The thing he's been avoiding since losing his job when he died. The sweet, tangy smell of the barbeque pit a few blocks away lures him forward, and not for the first time, he wonders what that job is like. Chris maneuvers around the outside of the crowds gathered at various spots along their path. There's something genuine about street performers without buckets for tips out in front of them. People simply do what they love for people who love it. Finding something to do forever is one of the few things people have to do in Purgatory, and Chris makes this decision like every other one he's made, by putting it off until something comes to him in a rapturous moment of clarity. Until then, Chris admires the others who know what brings them joy. For Chris, that will come at the end of all this in Heaven, with his wife. He hears the familiar embouchure of a trumpet.

*Maybe I could be a street performer. I like music.*

Chris watches at the back of a crowd as a man balances chairs on his chin. He studies the people's faces, both performers and audience, seeing the happiness in all directions. For a moment, he believes *he* could do this forever, not chairs on the face, but maybe a street musician…if having an interest in music was all it took to play an instrument. He had played trumpet in the junior high band, but that won't do.

Chris continues down the sidewalk, where storefronts reach up to the sky, because the stores are also apartments. Placing apartments above each building allows everything to be closer. Purgatory Enterprises is nothing if not spatially efficient. He passes a cookie store, thankful he doesn't live in those apartments. He lives over a bar and the sour smell of beer is often a deterrent after a long night. Cookies don't have that effect, not on Chris anyway. One can easily walk from one side of Purgatory to the other in only an hour or two. But that doesn't leave a lot of room to spread out. Even the streets are full of people. That means Chris spends a lot of time in his bedroom, alone with his thoughts. The street performers are the only ones that get space. Everyone gives them ample room, making the distance between the people on the street that much narrower. A woman singing something high-pitched and loud—something classical Chris assumes—receives a cheer from the other people on the sidewalk. A human statue takes this opportunity to change his position next to her to a faux operatic pose with a wide mouth and hands reaching to the sky.

Chris stops at the corner of the street outside the Crossroads bar. Along the facade there is a long bulletin board. On it there are hundreds of papers held up by pins. These boards are along many of the buildings. They are known as Scare Boards. These papers are assignments put up by the Guild for people who aren't going to die but have a near death experience. It is a moment of revelation in which the chauffeurs can make a change. This is another trial run feature of Purgatory Enterprises. These usually last long enough for someone to completely ruin it, and they never come back. There is a paper pinned up on the top row, the second one from the right, that Chris always seems to linger on as though it was a beacon. He's afraid that taking it will irrevocably chain him to it. It will force him to act on it. A firebreather blows a massive flame at the feet of an audience. The crowd moves away, shoving him like the tide toward the door of the bar. He hurries away from them.

Chris opens the door to Crossroads. He waves to Aditi sitting in a booth at the far, far corner of the bar, near the stairs to the apartments. A brilliant smile blazes across her golden-toned face. Her hand combs her thick black hair away from her eyes. Chris makes his way through the patrons to their usual booth. Over all the conversations, over racket of the bar, even over the band's soundcheck, Aditi shouts with perfect clarity, "I'm on the chopping block, baby!" She holds her beer to the sky.

That rebel yell means a chauffeur earned her place in Heaven. The bar erupts in a cheer.

Over the microphone, Elvis—or more likely a very committed impersonator, he's been there so long no one really knows at this point—congratulates the lady in the corner booth and gets "the show on the road."

Aditi gestures at the chilled beer bottles on the table across from her. "That's right, I'm out." She slaps an envelope and a score sheet on the cover of her copy of *Romancing a Monster: My Phlebotomist is a Vampire, Book 2 of the Hellfire Moon Saga*.

<u>Average Rank</u>: **9.5**
<u>Official Score</u>: **10**

"Well, you squeaked one in there," Chris says. He raises his voice to be heard over the rockabilly coming through the speakers. "Happy for you. I'm next." He adds his own review, and they clink beer bottles.

Aditi drinks until her bottle is empty. She bangs it down on the table and gestures to the bartender for another. She says, "Fuck, I can't wait to get out of this place and into Heaven."

"What a weird thing to hear from a Satanist."

"We were all wrong." She taps his leather bracelet with the star of David branded onto it with her bottle of beer and holds it up for him. He clinks her empty bottle. "Besides, you'll be right behind me. Oh, before I forget. There was a postcard in my mailbox. Apparently, they filled Sylvia's room already."

"That was quick."

"It was a transfer," Aditi says, flipping through her papers on the bench beside her. "Had a weird name. I couldn't tell if it was a girl or boy."

A waitress with short black hair and no back pockets brings her another round and a shot—on the house. Aditi downs the shot and starts on the bottle of beer with one hand, leaving the empty shot glass on the tray with the other. The waitress takes her eyes off Aditi only long enough to wink at Chris. As she dances through the crowd,

Aditi's eyes follow her away. Chris barely notices this ritual anymore. The band kicks into "A Little Less Conversation."

"Have you put anymore thought into what you want to do forever?" Aditi says, taking a swig from her bottle. "Or at least until you want to transfer to a new job. You know the first thing you have to do is fill out one of those cards."

"I know, I know," Chris says. "I'm not a big sports guy, so coaching doesn't seem to fit me like it does you. Maybe you can coach me. You'll have eternity. And you'll need it. I'm almost starting to hope I get removed before I have to decide. Maybe they'll just shove me in some office somewhere."

"Whoa, removed? You gettin' soft on me, boy?" Aditi accused. She sees a real sadness in his eyes. Her head tilts sympathetically. "There are only three ways to get removed." She ticks each one off on her fingers. "Lie. Flop. And tell someone how they're going to die. You telling me you're going to start breaking rules? Especially since following rules is the only thing you'll make a decision about. Also, it'd be shitty for me if you did that, so don't."

"I don't know," Chris takes a drink. "I just want to see Andrea. She'll help me figure it out when I get there."

"Speaking of which." Aditi leans forward, lacing her fingers together. "I saw the postcard. I don't think they're going to let her come."

Chris deflates. Part of him knew this was the most likely reality. "How'd you know that's what I was thinking?"

"Are you kidding?" She watches him accusingly from under her thick bangs. "I hear you at night. We share a wall. When was the last night you didn't cry yourself to sleep, kissing your pillow and calling her name."

Chris falls back against the booth. "Oh, come on. I'm not that loud. But seriously," he leans forward. "You don't think she'll come?"

"I don't think they'll let her come," Aditi says. She points the neck of her beer at him. She brushes her hair away from her neck and angles it—as she always does when the waitress with the short black hair and no back pockets is working—and says, "What do I always say? I say don't waste your time chasing ghosts. All you're apt to get is haunted. We've talked about that. Death is just the line in the sand between two lives that have nothing to do with one another. First it separated her life and yours, now it's separating your first life and this one." There must be something on Chris's face telegraphing his thoughts, because she quickly walks it back. "Look, you've been here too long. Hell, you're a ten away from being on the elevator out of here. They won't waste the time when you're right on the other side of it. Plus, you don't want your first time seeing her to be here. Do it at home. In private, so no one gets hurt."

"You're right," Chris says. "I just don't want to be stuck here like Ulie Lebenov."

"Wait," Aditi stops and turns back to the book. She opens the cover and inside there is an orange postcard. "Where did you hear that name?"

"A Little Less Conversation" ends, and the patrons bellow a unison cheer. Before the crowd has a chance to quiet, Elvis—or probably a very, very convincing impersonator—sings the story of a party that the warden had thrown back in the 50s.

"He's kind of notorious for being at Purgatory Enterprises longer than anyone else," Chris says. "I'm surprised you haven't heard of him."

"I don't really talk to people," Aditi says. "I'm kind of focused on moving on. I wouldn't talk to you and Sylvia if I didn't live with you. I'd just watch basketball and go to my room until the mail comes." She drops the postcard on the table for the two of them to read. "Ulie Lebenov. He's meeting me here, and I'm showing him up to the suite. You don't think *I'm* supposed to train him, do you?"

"Poor guy's been through training before," Chris says reading the rest of the postcard. "He's been here for years."

One by one the instruments on stage quickly fall silent. The music comes to an unplanned close, and the crowd in front of the stage backs away. A woman in acid washed jeans and a black tank top stumbles in her heels and knocks the beer out of Chris's hand. He slides against the wall to avoid the spill and to move away from her. The woman apologizes, but a commotion drowns her out.

"It's fine," Chris says. "I'll get a tow—"

The waitress comes out of the crowd with a damp towel. She mops up the spill with it, bending unnecessarily far over the table. She smiles at Aditi and Chris, then vanishes back into the crowd. "She's going to get one of us," Aditi says. Her eyebrows bounce.

Chris hears the rumbling of a fight breaking out. A small man screams up from chest-level of a much larger, ganglier person. The tall man's hands are so big Chris thinks the man could probably grab the other's entire head in it. The man's feet are huge, his body is huge, his face is huge. His hair is the color of dust, and his blue eyes are set deep in their sockets. The way he is dressed—an orange and white striped polo, blue jeans, and a woven leather belt—gives him a large childlike quality. Chris moves toward the scuffle yelling, "Whoawhoawhoa!"

The crowd pulls the two men apart. But really it looks more like they're pulling a chihuahua off a Great Dane. The man is small even to a person of an average height.

"I am sorry," the large man says. His booming Russian accent easily fills the bar. Chris assumes that this is Ulie Lebenov. "You knock the drink from my hand. Was accident."

The other man jabs a finger into Ulie's chest. "We're trying to have a good time, and you pour beer on my head."

Ulie timidly looks around at all the faces staring at him. "I do not mean to."

Chris pulls Ulie away from the man. "Come on, bud. Let's have a drink."

"Who the fuck are you?" the man screams. A sudden burst of white hot rage surges through Chris, but before he can act on it, the man kicks Chris away and slugs Ulie on his huge chin. His big head snaps backward, the rest of his body toppling onto Chris, who does little more than slow his descent.

"Now let's be cool out there," Elvis—maybe—says into the microphone.

The crowd swarms the man and brings him away from Ulie. He shouts for them to let him go, and reluctantly they do.

Chris anxiously slides out from underneath Ulie. Aditi helps him to his feet. "What the hell is your problem?"

"I'm sorry," the red-faced man says, pushing the other patrons away and smoothing his stretched-out t-shirt. "I'm just stressed out."

"What do you have to be stressed out about?" Aditi shouts.

Ulie wobbles upright, holding his chin. "He hit me," he says, fighting off tears.

"It wasn't about you," Aditi says. "Some people just have small dicks." She glares at the man as though leaches are sucking on his face. She motions to the waitress for another round and points to the big guy. "Let's get you some booze for that chin."

"Why he hit me?"

When Chris is certain the drama has ended, he turns from the angry man, who looks to Chris more like the one who caught one on the chin. He slips into the booth next to Aditi. "The famous Ulie Lebenov, I take it?"

"I am Ulie," he says with a big grin. His face is shadowy, but he sways happily to the music playing from the stage.

"I'm Chris, this is Aditi."

"Hello," Ulie says, still grinning. "I am to be meeting a person called Aditi."

"Mission accomplished," Aditi says.

Chris asks, "Were you American?"

"No," Ulie says. He looks at his big hands. "I die in America. When you die in America you go to the American Purgatory. I do not speak English until I die. Everything I learn, I learn from here."

"How'd you die so young?" Aditi says. "I'm always up for a funny story."

"Explosion for work."

Aditi laughs. Then she jerks her thumbs to herself. "Suicide. Well, it was an accident. They thought it was suicide. Some of the teachers assumed I was a bad day away from chewing shotgun pellets, I guess because I never went to church and always wore black. I was a basketball coach, at small high school with no equipment manager. I always stayed late to clean up. Bit of a neat freak. One night I was dumping the rock climbing ropes, and jerseys, and cardio bands down a laundry chute to be cleaned. I couldn't see where I was going, and a loose free weight tripped me up, and…" She whistles through her teeth and mimes one hand smacking down on top of the other.

"*Bozhe moy*," Ulie exclaims.

"Nah, it's not the funniest one I've ever heard." She leans back with her bottle turned up. She wipes her mouth with the back of her hand and scratches her ribs.

Chris changes the subject before it's his turn to talk about how he died. Maybe it's the innocence in Ulie's eyes, or maybe it's some leftover pull to perform one last mitzva, but Chris feels compelled to help this man. It could be those things, but in a part of his mind Chris is afraid to fully face, he knows it's because he doesn't want his wife to be the only thing calling his attention for the next few weeks.

And with Aditi leaving, there's not much else to focus on. "Well Ulie, she's on the chopping block. I just got my second ten. If anyone can help you get out of here, it's us."

Wonder stretches across Ulie's face. "*Blargodaryu vas*, thank you. My friends."

Two men enter the bar. The silence that follows is disorienting. The whiteness of their suits makes their skin a gaunt olive color by comparison. Their hair is perfectly coiffed as if made from the same mold. The smiles on their faces do not reach their eyes, but sincerity coats the words they speak. "You can all go back to what you were doing."

"Yes, we will only be here for a few moments." The two men approach the angry man who kicked Chris in the gut. "Please, continue with your debauchery."

"Son of bitch," Ulie says under his breath.

"That's right, Ulie," Chris says. His face twists in confusion. "Son of bitch."

Chris stands from the booth, and Aditi follows. "Hang tight," she says.

Chris hurries across the dancefloor. "Hey, hey," Chris says, in a deliberately nonchalant manner. "It was just a misunderstanding. No need to take anyone anywhere." Chris puts his hand on one of the men's shoulder. A feeling, not exactly regret, but more like the feeling a person might assign to an audible gasp, surges through Chris. He pulls his hand away as the man turns to him. "You know what, I don't think that needs to be there."

"There are reasons for a person's removal," the man says. The cheerfulness in his voice is still there, but it still hasn't quite made it all the way to his eyes. "Lying to a client. Sabotaging a job for a low score. Revealing a client's cause of death. Mr. Gage had committed one of these acts. He will now be removed from Purgatory Enterprises."

The other man in a suit lifts Mr. Gage from the barstool like he would a blowup doll and lays him across his shoulder with no further struggle. Chris watches the two men leave out a back door with shocked, open-mouthed silence. The sounds of the bar weakly return.

"Whoa, momma," Elvis says. "We're gonna take a quick break."

The screech of feedback blares as the band members quickly leave the stage.

"So much for the celebration." Aditi says.

Her voice comes to Chris as if through syrup, muffled and muddy. She gets a towel from the bartender. He hears the door to the bar open and sees Henry, the man who trained Chris after orientation, standing in the door holding a piece of paper. The seventy-year-old face he remembers looks like a young fifty, but he's still recognizable in his dirty blue jeans and heavy camo jacket.

"I'm gonna go upstairs," Aditi says. "Bringing him. You coming?"

"Be up in a second." Chris greets Henry with a hearty Wisconsinite handshake. "What are you doing here?"

"It's taking you too long to get out of here," Henry says. His smile is wider, and his face is somehow smoother. "It's like you *want* to be here."

"I was in a barfight tonight." Chris straightens with feigned pride. He stares in amazement at the youth beaming from his old friend. The once white beard and hair is now salt-and-peppered. "You look outstanding, bud."

"The longer you're there, the better you get. You looked like you saw a ghost when I came in. What happened?"

"Someone just got removed."

"Oh geez," Henry says. "That your first time to see it, huh? Uffda."

The slow wave of realization falls on Chris. "You've already gone to Hell. I didn't think they let people back in if they don't work here."

"You heard about the new visitation policy?" Henry hands over the piece of paper. "My wife is coming up. They're letting me meet her in the orientation center."

"Congratulations." Chris takes the piece of paper. There is the general information that accompanies every client's sheet, but for Charlotte Thames, there are notes scrawled in the margins and on the back. Hobbies, interests, kids' names, important moments, and right at the bottom is how she will die. Chris cringes.

"Thought I'd give you an easy ten to put you on the chopping block. She's the kind that'll give anyone a ten. Might as well be someone going to Heaven. I'm gonna get back to the center. The line is around the building." Henry claps Chris on the shoulder and shakes his hand. "Just bring up the kids. Remind her about the shampoo hunting story I told you. She'll be putty. See you on the other side, kiddo."

"It's good to see you, Henry."

Chris drops his hand and crosses the bar to the stairs. The swinging door glides open on its hinge. Muscle memory takes over for the four flights, allowing Chris to read the client information. He recalls the shampoo hunting story, not quite understanding it—he was too wary of ticks and Lyme disease to ever go hunting when he was alive—and memorizes the important notes Henry has added. The sounds of each floor ebb and flow around him in echoing waves as he climbs up and past each floor rising.

He hurries down the fifth-floor hallway to suite 5B. When he enters, Ulie and Aditi are going over a plan for his next client on the red Naugahyde couch. There is a description printed out and unfolded on the coffee table.

Chris holds up a finger when Aditi sees him and continues to his room. The walls are the light blue of robin eggs and are bare. His bed has red sheets and a royal blue comforter. A plain lamp rests on the wooden nightstand. In the corner is an old recliner next to a small desk. There is an empty file tray labeled "Clients" in red ink on masking tape. Chris lays Charlotte's file in the tray and sits in the chair. Aditi knocks on the door.

"Is everything—"

Chris closes his eyes and feels the air cool his skin.

# Chapter 2
## WE SPEAK THROUGH THE DEER

Chris opens his eyes to the vastness of the Wisconsin wilderness around him. The sheer cold stings. The sky is a cool blue behind clouds purple with rain, as the sun begins its trek across the sky. The light illuminates the haze of the morning through the trees like a sheer curtain. A lumbering bear moseys slowly through the dark woods, and a deer bolts in the opposite direction. Chris is sitting in a tree stand fifteen feet up, giving him a welcomed feeling of distance that he rarely gets at Crossroads. Distance from the growing crowds of strangers. Being this high off the ground, and this far from the nearest stand, he can rest easy. He wishes he had known about places like this when he and his wife were still alive. His breath plumes from his mouth.

Chris settles into this moment. That's all it is really, a moment. No matter how long he takes—even though this will only take a few minutes—in reality, the only time that will pass is a blink. Not even a second. Because this is the moment when Charlotte's life flashes before her eyes. The moment of death. Chris—if he wants his final high score, anyway—will walk her through each of the happiest moments she lived. With any luck this will be the last time he has to do this. He is in Charlotte's mind. Living in her final moment. He feels the warmth of Charlotte's soul.

A scared voice calls to him from below him. She's standing at a nearby tree where there is another stand fifteen feet from the ground. Charlotte is small and her wispy white hair reaches out of a camouflage toboggan. Her pink, aged face is the only thing not bundled in heavy camo. The pockets in her jacket bulge.

"Hi Charlotte. I'm Chris. A friend of your husband's."

"Henry? You look so young. I don't think you're s'pose'ta sit in another guy's stand. I'm no hunter, so you get a free pass this time."

"That's okay," Chris says. "I'm no hunter either."

"Well, that's for sure. You have my granddaughter's shoulders. Shoot a gun powerful enough for a deer and you'll blow yourself in half. What are you doing here?"

"Henry asked for my help with something. No one will know I was ever here. Promise."

Charlotte pauses. "How did you know Henry?"

"We work together."

"You worked at the plant?"

"Nah," Chris says. "His new job."

Charlotte steps onto the stand. A rusty screw snaps, jostling the stand, and Charlotte latches onto the tree trunk. She grabs at her neck where a sudden, stabbing pain flowers. It's fierce and comes so unexpectedly that she nearly topples off the ladder.

"You okay?" Chris stands. Charlotte drops her weight into the seat, breathing heavily. Chris waits to sit back down even though there is nothing he can do from here. "There we go. Be careful, I think I saw a bear. I may need you to protect me."

"Sorry, kiddo," she says. The pain in her neck is white hot but soon fades to a numbness that is almost rejuvenating. "When you get old, everything starts to hurt. What do you do, Chris?"

"Well, I help chauffeur people to the afterlife."

Charlotte falls silent. "Are you the Lord?"

"Nope. It's just Chris. No 'T.' And I'm not the devil either, so don't worry about that. But we don't have to talk about that. I'm just here to let you do something, anything within reason, before we go."

"So, I'm going to die today?"

"Yeah, but I mean, that's, like" Chris pauses to calculate. "The third most interesting thing that's going to happen to you today. I'm here to make things more enjoyable. So, what do you want to do?"

"Well, I'm already here," Charlotte says, gesturing to the sunrise. She rubs her arthritic hands together. "I've done enough. No use making a whole ordeal. You aren't gonna kill me, are you?"

"No," Chris says, holding his arms up. "I'm not really dressed for that."

"That's fine then. You can stay." Charlotte agrees.

"Tell me something," Chris says, leading her to the first moment she'll be reliving. "Why are there two stands right beside one another?"

"Henry always liked to bring someone with him," Charlotte says. Her voice slows, the way their voices always slow as the memory flashes before their eyes. "He would take one of our girls with him. Usually when Liz would stay at her friend's house, Katy would get up and going with him. Liz never liked it. Katy was our little tomboy. Got any kids, Chris?"

"Ew, no." Chris's face scrunches up in disgust. "No offense. My wife, Andrea, and I didn't really want them. She used to do this thing where if we heard a crying baby, she'd pretend to be blown away by the power of its wails. I'd pick up her legs when she grabbed a light pole or street sign, so it looked like she was completely blown away."

"You two kooks," Charlotte says.

"There was this one time we took a trip to New York City, and a kid was walking in front of us with his mom. He stops. The mom gets this mortified look on her face. The kid looks up at her like he saw a ghost. Even we stopped walking. Then the kid says, 'I'm gonna poop my pants.' So the mom snatches him up and sprints down the sidewalk. The kid just kept repeating it 'I'm gonna poop my pants. I'm gonna poop my pants until they were out of sight. We never heard anything. Never saw them again. It was a little disappointing. You know, closure and all."

Charlotte shakes her head with a gloved hand over her eyes.

"Every now and then when the house was too quiet and neither of us had said anything in a while, she'd turn to me and ask, 'Do you think he did it?' and we'd laugh. Didn't matter if we were fighting or sleeping or whatever." Time spins out as the wilderness brightens. Chris finds comfort in the silence that follows. The massive black bear lumbers across Chris's view a few dozen yards in front of them. Chris brings the conversation back to the kids. Their first steps, their first words, even their first children. And when her heart warms, Chris can feel it.

"Where-about are you from, Chris?"

"Chicago," Chris says. He's watching the bear sniffing at a tree. She doesn't see it, and she won't. And the only reason he does is because he is looking for it.

"Cripes!"

"You're not gonna give me shit like Henry, are you?"

"Alls I know is Henry was a good man. A good man, a great friend, and a better husband. And friends don't let friends be Bears fans."

"In my defense, I wasn't all that interested until I met my wife."

"No one's that good in bed, Christopher." Charlotte reaches into her coat pocket and comes out with two foil-wrapped sloppy joes. They were only lightly smushed from her near fall. "Hungry, kiddo?"

"I'm fine, but thanks," Chris says. The smell of cooked meat wafts over to him.

"I've got two if you change your mind."

"So, you come here twice a week to have a sloppy joe?"

"How'd you know that?" Charlotte asks, her mouth mostly full. She sips her Schlitz to wash it down.

"Well, you do, don't you?"

"It was Henry's favorite place in the world," she says, taking another bite. "He'd get up at four in the morning, and we'd have two joes and beer before he left. He'd do that a couple, two/three times a week after he retired. I talk too much. I get too hungry. You can't eat when you here to hunt. They smell it. Runs the deer off. You do good enough to hide your natural smell."

"Huh...never thought about that."

"Oh sure," Charlotte says, burping. "Shoot, you learn a lot about hunters being married to one as long as I was. He always said to watch the deer. 'Nature's dangerous, but she talks to us. We speak through the deer.' They'll tell you where other hunters are, where threats are. They'll even tell you how inexperienced a hunter is by where they don't go. If a group of them start running one way, then you talk too much, or smell too much, or there's something bad over there. Tells other hunters where to look, or where to look out. They know everything you do out here."

"Tell me about Henry," Chris says. "He ever bring you up here?"

"Once," Charlotte smiles at the memory to herself.

"Tell me about it."

"We were probably your age. Waking up that early is hard to do with two kids."

"I imagine," Chris says, staring into the haze of the morning. This is the story that Henry told him to bring up, and now all he can think of is the smell of Andrea's shampoo. The way he could always tell whether she had left for work with a simple inhale. He never realized how important that sweet flowery, cucumbery aroma was to his life until she was gone. He can even see the green and pink bottle through the steamed glass of their shower from the bed.

"The kids were at their grandmother's," Charlotte says around the last of her first sloppy joe. She even starts chewing slower. "I had asked him for weeks, I said, 'Henry, why don't I go with you? You go out in the woods all the time, I want to see that part of your life.' He'd go on and on about how it's no fun, but finally he agreed. So, I got up early as you please, got cleaned up and dressed, then cooked some joes. That's the tradition. So, we sit and eat. I could tell something was different. He wasn't quiet when he ate, and that was odd cause Henry always got in a zone. Laser focus, you know.

"We drove to the lodge. We started hiking, and he'd point out all the mistakes the other hunters made. 'Oh see there. That feed is too close to the lodge, they'll never eat that,' or, 'See how that feed is kind of spread out all over the place? That means they don't like it.' or 'Look at the prints! That's a six-point for sure!' and so on. He got so excited, and alls I saw was a bunch of deer food and holes in the mud." Charlotte pauses, sipping her beer. "We were up in that tree for, I don't know, forty-five minutes. I lean over and whisper, 'Are they coming?' and you know what he says?"

"No," Chris says, fibbing. "What did he say?"

"He says, 'No, they aren't coming. They probably won't come back here for a while.' I ask, 'well, how do you know that, Henry?' and you know what he says?"

"Your shampoo," they say in unison.

"That's right," Charlotte said. She looks down at her hand, flexing as though the fingers are already going numb. "So, I asked if he knew we weren't going to find any deer, then why did he go through everything else. Why did we spend an hour waiting for something that wouldn't come? He says, 'you wanted to see what it was like, so here we are. And I wanted to just sit with you for an hour. In the quiet.' They say when you lose someone it's like an emptiness, like there's a hole in you. If it was empty you wouldn't hurt so much. Really it feels like your heart is hungry. Just wants to eat. Wants to love. But everything you put in front of it—boil it in beer, fry it, don't matter—it just won't eat. Worst feeling in the world."

Chris remembers all the silly things he used to do to get a smile out of Andrea. All the mornings he had tied up his hair in a towel and listened to her gossip and vent while she got ready for work. All the horror movies he had watched through wincing eyes on her behalf and yelped like a puppy when the jump scares suddenly jolted him. How many times had that made her quietly giggle next to him on the couch? The number is lost among the countless other memories of the things he only did because she wanted him to. He thinks of her pale face looking up from the hospital bed. Thinking of her always leads to this. To the way she looked before she died. "This is pretty great. I would love to spend a few quiet hours with my wife here."

"Why don't you bring her here?"

"I'm working on it," Chris says. "I have to get to Heaven first."

"What do you mean?"

"She died," Chris says. "Five years ago."

"Cripes, kiddo. I'm so sorry. Never had kids, I'm assuming?"

"No," Chris says. "Eventually, Andrea changed her mind. It was something we fought about for a while. It was the only decision I ever really made. We even got an old rescue dog first. Little fat pitbull. Named her Waffles."

"Did you relent?" She is watching him now.

"I did. Three months after we started trying, nothing good happened. She started having pains, so we went to a doctor. She had ovarian cancer. A year later it was over. Everything was. They caught it too late. If I hadn't fought her so long on the issue, we could've found it in time. There's something worse than losing someone, and it's watching something slowly take them away from you. Piece by piece. And then living with the fact that you're glad it's over so you don't have to see her hurting anymore."

"Did you tell her you love her?"

"Yeah, of course."

"Then don't go boo-hooin' just cause you were being yourself. It's over, kiddo. Marriage isn't a one-person-takes-all agreement. She dragged you to all those Bears games, she could wait a year for a kid."

Chris laughs quietly. "I'm supposed to be making you feel better, you know that, right?"

Charlotte finishes the joe. "You know, I could tell you weren't a hunter. Got those regular shoes on, and you aren't in camo or orange. You're from Chicago. I'm willing to bet you almost fell off that stand before you got comfortable."

"And circle gets the square," Chris says.

"I'm not saying you are an angel or what have you."

"I'm probably more of a ghost than anything else now that I think about it."

"And you knew Henry. I'll give you that. Tell me something one time..."

She wants proof that he's telling the truth. Chris doesn't think he would have to be dead to know that. "Charlotte, do you remember how I said you dying will be the third most interesting thing to happen today? Well, the most interesting thing today is that you are going to see your husband," Chris says, "I didn't even get that. I know I'm just some guy in a tree, so you don't have to believe me. I didn't believe it when it happened to me. But I can prove it. The last thing Henry said to you was that he was going to see the cats."

She looks down at her fingers. "I never told anybody that."

"He told me. Just like he told me that you two would smoke weed in the attic and occasionally use the smell as a reason to talk to the girls about not smoking weed. He knew that was the only way I could prove that this is real. He also says that Buttons misses you, and that even though it's counterintuitive, you can find him with the cats...and the better weed."

"Where's that?" Charlotte askes.

"You'll get to all that. It's a whole orientation thing."

Charlotte reached for her neck. She stands too suddenly, and the stand below her creaks. It shifts under her feet, and she stumbles. She latches onto the chair trying to steady herself.

"Be careful," Chris says. His voice is concerned, but his eyes are fixed on taking in the expanse before him. He leisurely stands and makes for the ladder.

Charlotte groans and her numb fingers come to her neck. They massage the pain, and she can feel the unevenness of the vertebrae, like gravel. Her legs fold. She reaches for the ladder. "Chris, can you call someone? Something's not right."

"I'm sorry, Charlotte."

Charlotte moves toward the ladder, and the stand crumbles under her weight. She falls fifteen feet, landing on a root. The connection to her limbs is severed. Her vision blurs and begins to pinhole.

"Don't move," Chris says. "It won't hurt if you stay still."

Charlotte steels herself against the instinct to move.

"I think this is my favorite place on Earth too," Chris says. He sits down beside her. "So, thank you for showing me this. Even if you didn't mean to. Your vision will start to pinhole, and when it stops, we can go. But don't worry. When you open your eyes again, you'll be in a room with Henry. You might want to hurry though. That bear smelled your sloppy joes, and we'll want to be out of here before the second-most interesting thing starts happening to you."

# Chapter 3
## ICE CREAM

Chris stays in the chair for a moment, feeling the warmth of his body return beneath his tee shirt. He never actually left the room, only his mind went to the snowy Wisconsin forest. Or was it soul? He never considered this until now. The winter Midwestern air he breathed still waits in his chest. He doesn't open his eyes, because until he opens them, nothing begins again. He's still in the moment, one he wants to savor. It's the moment when he knows he has finished his last client before taking the elevator to Heaven. That thought alone warms the air in his chest. And now, the sight of his bare robin-egg-colored walls welcomes him back to the empty room. The breath of the Wisconsin forest pours from him.

"—alright?" Aditi finishes. She opens the door to the room, seeing the cold cloud of fog Chris releases from his lungs. He is wearing a smirk. She stops in his doorway, side-eyeing him. "Did you just get your third ten?"

Breathe, Chris calmly reminds himself. Just breathe. His vision readjusts to the light in the room. He's thinking of his wife, of seeing her for the first time in years. He imagines walking into the house she picked out for them when they were alive, Waffles bouncing at the door—he can almost hear her paws scratching at it—yipping. He'll let her out into the back yard and follow the hallway to the bedroom. He'll smell her shampoo and hear the water running, and he'll sit on the edge of the bed, waiting for her. He tells Aditi, "I think I just got on the chopping block."

"You're really stealing my thunder, man. Come on. I'm trying to help him with his next client before I go back." Aditi grabs his hand and pulls him out of the chair to his feet, leading him to the small living room outside his door. The apartment is bare. There are three bedrooms and a kitchen. Between Chris's bedroom door and Aditi's, a table with a flat screen TV stands facing a black coffee table and red Naugahyde couch. To the right of the couch there is a lamp and a door to a third bedroom. Ulie is peering down at the coffee table, and Aditi drops down beside him on the couch. The television is off, so for once there are no distractions.

"Okay, so what's the scoop?" Chris leans over the living room coffee table to peer down at the description from an upside-down aerial view as Aditi reads aloud. The client's name is Arthur. A retired fishing captain. Weird job, Chris thinks, marking that one off his mental list of possibilities. The open ocean is one of his biggest fears. Heaven can get its fish from someone else, thanks. Chris remembers to pay attention then. Arthur's last moments will come at his wife's wake. It's his heart. The family will tell people it's a broken heart, but really, it's a cardiac infarction. His mind returns to the posters in the mailroom, the ones that list the areas of review. The most difficult section of the feedback survey to score high on is Connection. The chauffeurs must literally find a way to connect to a stranger who is dying in the blink of an eye. That's the key. If a chauffeur can ace Connection, the rest of the score is basically sealed.

Chris sets off mining for a simple connection between the client and Ulie. Then it hits him, he doesn't really know anything about Ulie. He's heard stories. But until a few minutes ago, he'd never actually met the guy. "How can we connect you to this guy? Tell me about yourself."

"I am Ulie."

"Sure," Chris says, waiting for more. "But, why do you want to go to Heaven?"

"I see," Ulie says. His large face sags. "My ma. I came to America for better life. I make special explosions for Hollywood movie. I try to save money. Bring her to America. She die before I return." Aditi slides her arm around his shoulder and squeezes. She looks at Chris with her version of puppy-dog dramatics and a pitiful, pouting bottom lip. If only she could cry on command to really bring the look home.

"I think I'm starting to understand how you died," Chris says.

"Explosion for work."

"Right." Chris stands from the table. He claps enthusiastically. "Okay, I think we can work with that, bud. Come on, I'll go with you."

"You go with me?" His face brightens, and suddenly, he is a new person.

"Sure," Chris waves him toward the closest bedroom. "They don't care if we tag team these things."

Ulie stands, picking the paper up off the table. In his gigantic hand, it looks like a postcard. Ulie walks to his new room, and much like Chris's bedroom, this room has a bed and a chair. Next to the chair is a small desk with a tray labeled "clients" with the masking tape and marker. The only difference between the rooms is rather than blue paint, Ulie's room is a dull mint green color. Ulie drops the paper into the tray and sits on the chair. Under his weight, the footrest springs upward, and the seat back falls into a reclining position. The recliner tips backward, and Aditi is ready to catch him before he topples over and bangs his head on the floor. Ulie is careful to keep at least one eye open. He taps his lap with both hands.

"Ulie, I've known you for thirty minutes. I'm not going to sit in your lap."

"Should I go alone?"

"No," Chris says. "I want to help."

"Then sit." He slaps his lap again.

"Yeah, sit in his lap," Aditi says nudging him with her shoulder. Her smile is twice as bright when she knows Chris is uncomfortable.

"Don't we have a sofa or a love seat?"

"What? You think he's going to bite you?" She nudges him again. Ulie quietly groans. He opens his left eye, and the right slams shut as if a kamikaze no-see-um chose this day to make a go at Goliath.

"It's just weird going from handshakes to laps so quickly," Chris says, walking to the side of the chair in search of a lever. "Why don't you just go? You said you wanted to help before you leave. Don't stand on the sidelines. Life's too short and all."

Aditi watches Chris feeling around the chair for a hidden lever or maybe a panel leading to one. "You know the Guild gets red-assed when people take jobs when they've already moved on. So, no."

"Well, can we at least lean the chair back up?"

"It's broken," Aditi says. "Even I couldn't sit in it without it flying backwards like that. You'd have to get out, then you'd both have to fall in at the same time. Would that be better?"

"Fine." Chris stands up. Ulie watches him with one eye. "What are you doing?"

"I wait for you," Ulie says, closing his left eye and opening his right. "If I close my eyes, I go alone."

"You can blink though," Chris says. Ulie nervously shakes his head. "Wait, why don't we use another chair?"

"There's no time!" Aditi playfully shouts, shoving Chris onto Ulie. "Go!"

When he falls, he and Ulie flinch, and Chris feels his equilibrium shift in the blackness of his closed eyes, like he is being taken by a wave. His arms naturally flail as he tries to stabilize himself. Slowly he feels his weight under his feet. When he peeks at where he is, taking a moment to adjust to this suddenly new version of light, he is standing in the middle of a visitation room in a chapel, flapping his arms to stabilize his balance. He is painfully aware that he looks like a man trying to take flight. That'll never work, he thinks to himself. I'll hit my head on the ceiling.

The room is small, and the chairs and tables are pushed to the perimeter wall. A thin rug the color of sand lies on top of the room's carpet the color of mud. A few tables along the walls, beneath the windows, along with two sofas and a love seat in the corner, sport a two-color, beige and off-beige floral pattern and very few stains for a public seating area. A few extra wooden chairs sit empty along the wall.

By the door is a flimsy plastic posterboard stand with a collage of pictures of the woman of the hour. Unlike the room, the collage is colored with bright pink and green letters saying, "We love you Mira" at the top, and the dates of her life at the bottom. Her husband, Arthur, was a soldier in a war which, based on the pictures, had taken place in black and white. During what Chris deduces is the 1970s from the flower-patterned clothing and medallion, she owned a daycare center called The Sunny Playground, and Chris can't help but notice the thick clouds in the sky in the picture. They had an enormous family, only about eleven or twelve of whom are present now. The room is long and narrow as if to make a path for the silver coffin at the far end of the room, and for now everyone is huddled in the center of the room around Arthur.

As Chris looks around them, he can see a clear divide in the generations which came after her. Her two sons, their son and daughters, and their sons and daughters. The youngest daughter is holding a baby that has the very same cheeks of the woman in the black and white photos. The room is quiet. Not like a library, but like a church when the organ stops, and the priest is walking to the pulpit. People are talking but quietly, as though to not interrupt any conversations between the mice in the walls. Two of Mira's granddaughters are standing at the coffin, and Chris can see them changing the glasses that Mira is wearing.

One of them says, "they just don't look right."

"Lisa, the ones you put on her are reading glasses," the other growls through her clenched teeth. "She can't wear reading glasses when she's not reading. She just looks stupid."

Arthur is a small man with almost no hair left. His back is hunched from a lifetime of punishment at the hands of time. Brown spots freckle his head and shaky hands in irregular shapes and sizes. He's wearing denim jeans, and a green and navy-blue plaid shirt buttoned up to the center of his chest. The top splits to give breathing room for the patch of wiry, white hair peeking out about the neck of the tank top he wears underneath. His gapped smile is wide, but the bloodshot eyes above it are sad. One by one his family slips away to the coffin or out of the room. Eventually everyone congregates in the lobby, leaving Arthur alone with his wife.

Chris feels a tap and spins to see Ulie's large happy face smiling so wide that Chris notices his drastically crooked canine tooth. Chris looks down at Ulie's hands where he holds two cartoonishly tall ice cream cones, one chocolate and one vanilla.

"I was not expecting this," Chris says.

"What do I do?"

"I'm guessing you should wait until after to get ice cream."

"Nyet, with him." Ulie gestures to the old man standing at the head of the coffin. "How do I start? I am nervous with you watching."

"Well don't be nervous," Chris said, watching the ice cream defy gravity atop the cones. "Just do what you normally do, and we'll adjust. I'll be here to spot you. Start with a joke. I always say 'Hi, I'm Chris. No, no 'T,' just Chris. It's a dumb joke but a good icebreaker."

"Blagodaryu vas. Thank you, thank you, Christopher." Ulie hugs him, and Chris nearly topples backwards as though a mattress has fallen on him. "You are my friend."

"Just remember," Chris pushes him to arm's length. "He's a family man. So, think of your mother. Try to channel that."

"I do," Ulie says, walking away.

"Hey, real quick," Chris says, tugging on Ulie's elbow. "When you said you made special explosions, what does that mean?"

"Ice cream melt," Ulie says, gesturing toward Arthur. "One minute."

"Yeah, no, yeah get after it, sorry." Chris watches him saunter to the small man.

"Hello, Arthur," Ulie says. "Ice cream?"

"No, thank you." Arthur's voice is dry and trembles with old age. He glances at the cones as if to confirm what Ulie was asking, as if what he asked was so bizarre that a person could only truly believe it after seeing it.

Ulie looks back, licking both cones. Chris smirks and waves him on. "My name is Ulie," he tells Arthur.

"Ulie," he says with a nod. "I'm Arthur."

"No 'T,' just Ulie."

"No…" Chris says under his breath.

"Okay," Arthur says, confused. He watches Ulie, like a computer scanning for viruses. "Did you know my wife, Mr. Ulie?"

"I do not," Ulie says, licking at the dot of ice cream from the end of his nose. "I am here for you."

Chris grimaces. Had to be a better way of saying that.

An awkward moment passes between the two as Arthur's disbelief wrestles reality. "Are you a…are you foreign, son?"

Ulie somehow becomes taller with pride. "I am of Ufa, capital of Bashkortostan."

"Well, you sound Russian." Arthur's brow furrows at him. His cheeks flush. His thin white hair seems to glow in contrast to his darkening face. His left hand twitches. Chris can feel a strange tension mounting between them. "When I was in the Air Force, we didn't like Russians. Why are you here, son?"

"Because today you are to die."

Oh, no…Chris thinks as he readies himself for intervention.

"You're going to kill me?" Arthur's face slowly lengthens in exhausted dismay. He shambles square with Ulie. Arthur meets the large man's gaze with suspicion. His wild eyebrows point in all directions. "I'm a vet."

"I want to help you." Ulie says. His smile waivers.

"How dare you come here. What do you want? Secrets?" Arthur's face twists in a grimace. He suddenly looks like a cornered animal. He rubs absently at his chest. "I've been retired for forty years. I don't know anything. Can't you people leave me alone?"

"I—," Ulie stammers, backing away from the small man as he closes in. Both of their faces are turning red, Ulie's with embarrassment. "I—"

Chris hurries to the space between them. "Whoa there, bud. You gonna be good?"

"Get that man away from me!" Arthur points a damning finger at Ulie and wipes his eye. He winces and folds at the waist. "My Mira is dead! And you come here?"

"Hey, hey," Chris says, holding up his palms. "There's nothing we can't just talk through. This is not an occasion for fighting. Am I right? Let's have a seat." Chris gestures to one of the love seats near the wall.

"For fifty years," Arthur says, holding his chest, breathing heavily, coughing. He makes a point to stay where he is. "Help," he manages to whisper.

"Wait, are you talking about the Cold War?" Chris's face screws up in disbelief.

"I think so," Ulie says. "They always do."

"Fifty years," Arthur repeats.

"Breathe for me, alright?" Chris says. "This is not a place to fight. He's here to help you, and so am I. There's no Reds. No commies. No spies. We're just people."

Chris's eyes meet Arthur's. A very real—albeit irrational—fear is buried there. Arthur wipes his left eye with the back of his hand, sniffs. The redness in his face holds. He is still heaving breath. Chris's mind scrambles. Coming up with something to squash a lifelong prejudice doesn't come as naturally to him as making a joke in a tense moment. He doubts that will help right now. He returns—like he typically does in moments like these—to the posters hanging on the walls of the mailroom. The hardest section to get a good score on is Connection. He looks to Mira for some sort of sign. She's no help. Her reading glasses sit crooked on her nose, and Chris thinks the least they could've done was straighten them. His attention turns to the black and white picture of Mira and Arthur standing in front of a bus. Mira is wearing a white dress with flowing white sleeves and a belt wrapped around her waist. Arthur stands proudly in an Air Force coat with comically large breast pockets and buttons on each side. His polished black shoes seem to sparkle in the flash from across those sixty or seventy years of history. In the next picture, Mira is wearing bell bottoms and a plain yellow sleeveless shirt. Her hair is a sandy blonde straightedge that curtains down to her waist on either side of the flower pendant dangling from her neck.

"Look, Arthur," Chris says, reluctantly placing a hand on the small man's shoulder. "Mira wouldn't want you to be angry. Certainly not here. She would want you to find peace. Am I right?" The question was less rhetorical than it sounded. Chris never actually saw Arthur's description and was stabbing in the dark. Death can bring out the best in people though. "Remember those days? When she talked about peace for everyone?"

Arthur nods and relents. "I'm sorry. He said he was going to kill me though."

"To be fair," Chris says, pausing to think of an elegant, noncontroversial way to explain. "He didn't exactly say that. He just said you were going to die. He's not wrong."

"How does it happen?" Arthur says, wincing at the growing pain in his chest.

"We're not allowed to tell you," Chris says. "But you can probably guess."

"We do not mean to scare you," Ulie says, chocolate dripping from the cone over his gargantuan hand. "And if I can say, you are in a good place. Your wife. She is to be waiting for you. You see her soon."

"What does he mean?" Arthur says. He's rubbing the hair on his chest.

"You should talk to him," Chris says, sympathetically. He puts his other hand on Ulie's shoulder and squeezes. "I think he'll help you better than I can. He's a good guy."

"Dying," Ulie says. He bites the cone in half and continues to speak as he chews. "Is not so bad. Does not really feel like anything. Is warm. And then you feel nothing. No pain."

"What is this?" Arthur asks Ulie. His left eye is red from a burst vessel. He tries to wipe at it, but the weight of his arm is too much to lift and uses his right hand instead.

"Is truth," Ulie says. "You will die. Soon. But you have wife to meet you at next part. Me. Chris," he gestures toward Chris. "We must wait to see loved ones. You go through next part together. With Mira."

Chris backs away to let Ulie finish. The two talk like forgotten friends for a few minutes as Ulie finishes the last of his ice cream. Arthur's body language loosens as Ulie steers him through the happiest moments of Arthur's life. Ulie even makes Arthur laugh. As things wind down, Arthur offers his hand. Ulie looks to the hand and back to Arthur. The catcher's mitt-sized hand envelops Arthur's. Arthur's face slumps to the left. He drops to one knee.

"Is okay," Ulie says, helping Arthur to the floor. "Lie still. If you are still, you do not hurt. Just numb. Do not worry. They will call the hospital."

"Dad?" a voice calls from the hallway. "Dad!"

Chris closes his eyes and feels the gravity shift underneath him like diving into deep black water. Suddenly, he can feel himself falling. Not into water, but into a lap. His eyes spring open, as if from a dream, and he is lying over Ulie in the recliner.

"Well, how'd it go?" Aditi asks, standing over him.

"I think I'm beginning to understand why he's been here as long as he has." Chris stands up, using Ulie for support. Ulie giggles under his weight.

"What happened?" Aditi says. Her eyebrows raise in genuine interest.

"Turns out a lot of old Americans still have some opinions about the Cold War."

"Yeah," Aditi says. She grabs her copy of Romancing a Monster: My Phlebotomist is a Vampire and the leather jacket off the table. She put the jacket on, flipping her hair out of the collar. "I guess they would be dying now. Well, I helped, so I'm out. Just came back for my jacket. See you in a week or so?" She hugs Chris's neck, and he hugs her back. She pushes him away, suddenly. The muscles in her arm flex. It's something Chris has come to expect from her, so much so that he doesn't even stumble backward anymore. "Touch me again, and I'll have you removed, you understand? Ulie, good to meet you, sir. Don't take too long, okay?" She playfully slaps Chris on the face and walks out of the apartment, leaving them with the image of the phoenix on her back to remember her.

"Ulie," Chris says, feeling shame grip his stomach. "I'm sorry."

"You did nothing," Ulie says. "You help me."

"Maybe," Chris says. "I just didn't know, you know? People talk about you. I knew who you were before I met you earlier. It's not nice what people say. And I...I haven't done anything to shut that down."

"Is okay, buddy," Ulie bares his crooked teeth. His smile makes him look like a giant toddler. His bigness and adulthood drain away. "You did not know. Beside. This is why we are to be doing this. Compassion. Connection. Compassion, yes?"

"Yeah," Chris says, not feeling better about his part in the gossip. He put his arm around Ulie's shoulder. "We're gonna get you to Heaven, bud. What's with the ice cream, by the way?"

Ulie follows Chris to the living room. "Is nice. If you are about to die, would it not be better to hear with morozhenoye?"

Chris cannot help but to smile. "I'll give you that, I would rather have the ice cream. Listen, tell me about this explosion thing."

# Chapter 4
## THE WORST PART IS WAITING

Sitting at the foot of his bed, Chris wishes he could just go to sleep. The worst part of living on the Purgatory Enterprises campus isn't remembering death, not that his constantly intruding view of the blue sky surrounded by grass doesn't throttle his day. It isn't having to work, essentially, as a customer service representative for a person's death after a decade of being in human resources. No refunds here, bud. It isn't even watching people move on without him, although he can't wait for his own rebel yell. I'm on the chopping block, baby!

No, the worst part is waiting. It's waiting to get feedback, waiting to get to Heaven, waiting to see Andrea. And there isn't much to do in between clients. But that's not the point of working as a chauffeur. The point is to give people time to think. About their past life, about their next one, and Chris thinks about what he wants to do forever. He dithers between future careers in Heaven, between what Ulie calls "special explosions for Hollywood movie" (pyrotechnics technician), teacher, or maybe musician; but then again, he could go into criminal forensics. He could dust for fingerprints, why not?

Or maybe, it doesn't really matter right now. All there is in the world is getting that third ten and getting into his wife's arms. She'll help him figure it out from there. She did after college when a liberal arts degree didn't exactly hone his interests any further in the five years it took to get it. Andrea knew in middle school what she wanted, and nothing would justify deviation from her path into the world of robotics. She received a master's degree in the time Chris graduated undergrad. She had turned their basement into a workshop while Chris settled into a nine-to-five that, even without Andrea's help, would've left him living comfortably.

They travelled around the country on vacations that she'd planned—Niagara Falls, flipping the bird to Canada just because, Cherry Springs State Park in Pennsylvania to see the Northern Lights, Arizona to throw rocks across the Grand Canyon—marking off landmark after landmark until they were off to other countries. These are the moments that keep his mind occupied between mailbox runs. These moments are the closest he can get to dreaming.

When he closes his eyes, he can see her skewed reflection painting her face yellow in the fogged bathroom mirror. She had dyed her hair royal blue and wrapped it around rollers zip-tied and hair sprayed together in stacks on her head. Blue and yellow dots speckled the sink, countertop, and mirror. She wore a string of red golf balls around her slender neck, and a green throw blanket wrapped around her torso like a towel. She hummed The Simpsons theme in the high-pitched, cracked growl of Marge Simpson.

Chris finished shaving his face in the sink next to hers. His hair was dyed bright yellow and spiked in all directions. He pulled the pacifier out of his mouth, "I still don't see why I couldn't have been Marge."

"We both have hazel eyes. Yours are blue, dear. You can't have everything."

Chris tugged at his blue onesie, which despite its bagginess, was somehow tight and twisted everywhere on him. "Are you planning on carrying me?"

"You can walk," she pouted. "Don't forget your bow, Maggie."

Andrea handed him the yellow paint and clipped a small blue bow in his hair. She glanced at her watch. "The season premier starts in eight minutes. You better hurry." She took the pacifier out of his mouth again and kissed him and replaced it. There was something more Marge than Andrea about her. She walked out of the bathroom, as he rushed the yellow paint across his face.

"We should really have a party with more people if we're going to dress up," he called after her. "My hair looks fantastic. People should see it."

And then the memory changes. It always changes when a mind can't dream.

"Chris," her voice comes to him from the doorway, as cold and brittle as frost.

"I'm com—"

Chris stiffens at the sight of her withered body propped against the door frame. Her eyes are sunken into her skull beneath dirty purple rings. Her skin is thin and pale, and her bones jut out harshly around her body like a toothpick figure of a woman. Her hospital gown dangles off her bony shoulders. Bloody scabs are crusted where her fingernails should be, and her black hair surrounds her on the floor. Her hands tremble as she reaches for him.

"Honey, what am I going to do?" She falls to the floor.

The dull smack jolts Chris back to reality. This is what he sees every time he lets his mind wander.

He hears Ulie leaving the apartment, humming an Elvis song he can't quite peg.

Chris sits on the edge of the bed, and he waits. He wants to sleep, but he can't. Nobody can. And besides, this is not a time for that. It's a time for reflection. Chris is starting to believe that thinking about the lives of others is part of that reflection—all the lives he's watched end. He isn't supposed to chauffeur a person into the afterlife and walk away, but to consider their experience. Their death. But rather than sit and think about Charlotte or Lucas or the others, he is thinking about Ulie. About how long he's spent hopping from apartment to apartment, trying to find the right people to help him. Having to learn a new language. Chris has been without Andrea for years, but is that even a blink compared to Ulie's time waiting to ride the elevator to his mother? And why should Ulie have to sit in the chair, endless months and ice cream cones stacked like bricks in the wall between him and the rest of his existence? It isn't the ice cream. It isn't the crooked teeth or his bigness. All of that makes him so painfully innocent, harmless. There is the language barrier. Sure, but for years? It's basically under control now. Certainly, three people in a row, in all that time, would have found his goofy face and inability to communicate charming, or at the very least, sad. It's because people can't just let go of their prejudices. That's not something he's ready to accept. A sudden anger colors his face and heats his cheeks.

Chris thinks about his wife. He wants to tell her that his worst regret is not making a real family with her. That he never gave her what she wanted. He wants to say that she'll never want again. He wants to look her in the eyes and—

A knot burns in his stomach. He can't remember what she looked like. Not the way it was everyday anyway. He can only recall the tortured face the cancer left with her. Every time he thinks of her, the face that comes to him is of some woman outside a phone booth from a music video by some band in the 90s. His hands brush back his hair, and he stares at the floor. When had that happened? He feels betrayed, like something has been stealing his memories when he isn't looking.

Chris sits on the edge of the bed, thinking of his wife.

What am I going to do?

# Part 2
# Heaven (Formerly Bossier City)

# Chapter 5
## BURNIN' LOVE

Chris's high-tops squelch on the white tile floor in the foot-shaped puddles of water in front of his mailbox. "Folsom Prison Blues" plays quietly through the overhead speakers. As he starts his third attempt to dial the combination with nervous fingers, two skateboarders barrel from the Hell exit to the Heaven one, banging on the mailbox doors on either side of the corridor. Chris starts to run but jumps against the wall of mailboxes, and now he finds himself side-by-side with the couple who seem to be studying mouth-to-mouth dentistry. Chris groans loudly. He returns to the mailbox above the puddle of water.

Ulie approaches, pointing to the ground. "Why is wet?"

Chris looks at him and looks down. "Oh, it's—don't worry about it." He returns to the mailbox dial, but Ulie waves him off.

"No bother," he says shaking his head. He holds up a yellow mailing envelope. "Only the client papers come. Not feedback."

In the week since his last solo outing, Chris has learned a lot about life in Purgatory Enterprises. The first is that after a person has been here as long as Ulie, the turnaround for feedback delivery is much, much shorter. Roughly twenty-four hours. Ulie has chauffeured four people, and he has received feedback from three of those four people. Chris has received none. After working the kinks out with Arthur, he is confident that today Ulie will receive his second of three tens. He's even more confident that today will be the last day he'll have to check this mailbox. Despite Ulie's confidence, Chris quickly dials in the combination—now that the pressure is off, he has no trouble—and opens the small door to nothing but a universal blue and white sticker on the floor of the mailbox that says, "Check back for more updates from the Guild of Divinity." He deflates. Just in case, he leans closer to see all the way to the back of the box and only finds darkness.

"This person is not old," Ulie says. Chris turns to him, unsure of what he is talking about. He is staring at the piece of paper like it's covered with something sticky. He hands Chris the description of his next client.

The woman's name is Melanie. She is thirty-two and the way that her description reads is like an altered biography of his own life. Her boyfriend died young, and she never married. She threw herself into her health much like Chris had when Andrea died. Chris ran marathons, and Melanie got up to forty miles a day four times a week on her bike. The only difference seems to be that Melanie will already know what she wants when she arrives in Purgatory Enterprises. She had finished veterinarian school and started her own practice in only a decade.

Chris's heartbeat rises at the thought of the last run he took. His uncomfortable sneakers pounded on the dirt road. He smelled the damp woods around him. The Nirvana song thumped through his noise cancelling headphones, Kurt's angry, growling voice lead into the chorus of "Pennyroyal Tea." He felt a presence in front of him, and as he looked up, he saw a flash. Henry's voice told him not to move. It won't hurt if you don't move. Just enjoy the view, kiddo. Not a cloud in the sky.

He's brought back to the Purgatory mailroom when someone runs into him, shoving him into the wall of mailbox doors.

"Hey!" Ulie shouts. "Careful."

"Or what, comrade," the older man and his friend turn to Ulie. Looking up to Ulie's face, the men back down.

"Be nice," Ulie says. He glares at them as they back away much slower than they had approached. "Is why you are here."

"This one might be tough for you," Chris said, glancing at Ulie's large, but hardly fit physique. He hands the description back to Ulie. He closes his mailbox and starts toward the exit for Crossroads. "You can do it though."

"She is not sick," Ulie says, following.

"No, she's not," Chris says. He holds the door open for Ulie, who ducks under the frame. "You see that 'ET' in a circle next to her name?"

"Yes. I never have seen this before."

"You've never seen that before?" Chris reminds himself that Ulie didn't know English when he arrived at Purgatory Enterprises. "Sorry. The 'ET' means something like early transition…or maybe termination. I haven't gotten one either. I can't remember, but basically, they are killed. Either by health or by another person. Everyone under sixty gets it. I had one on my write-up. Even you probably had one."

Ulie drops his eyes to the bottom of the page where the cause of death is listed. "Oh no," he says. "They hit her but did not stop."

Chris maneuvers around the crowd gathered around the street performers. Music drifts through the air with the smell of barbeque. "You might not be able to use your ice cream move. Might have to ride a bike." Chris says, imagining Ulie riding a bike, like a bear on a tricycle in a circus, trying to talk to a stranger about how they are going to die.

"Oh, no."

"Yeah,"

"I never had a bike," Ulie says.

"Of course not." Chris rubs his eyes, trying to massage a plan to the front of his mind. He listens to the cheers and laughter of the people along the street. Chris initially equates a new sound to bagpipes, but only because he knows the instrument, whatever it is, is a little weird. Even the elderly couples sit on benches clapping in rhythm with the rest of the people. He recognizes the melody of "Hava Nagila" blaring out of the chambers of an accordion, not bagpipes. He sees the door of Crossroads and the white letters on the glass door that read: Bathroom is in the alley. "Oh, yeah. They have pit stop things on a bike trail, right? Just be at a rest area. Trust me, just make sure she knows that's she's not alone. That's what I wanted to know. Boom, there you go."

"With morozhenoye," Ulie says excitedly.

"Sure. People on bikes don't usually accept ice cream, but sure."

"More for me."

"You know, you can just eat ice cream, right? There's a place right there." Chris points to a small 50s-style ice cream shop with bright blue and pink lights along the walls of the white interior. The cashiers wear white paper hats, and sleeves rolled up to the elbows. Not for the first time, Chris wonders what serving ice cream for eternity might be like. Cold, he thinks.

Ulie snaps his big fingers in front of Chris's face. The sounds pop like pistol shots. "You think about being ice cream person again."

"It's coming down to the wire, bud. I have to start getting real about what I'm going to do." As the two of them cross the street to Crossroads, the Scare Board catches his eye. He stares at the yellowing piece of paper on the top row, second from the right. "But for now, I think I can really help you hammer this home."

"I have had two tens before," Ulie says. His lip twitches very slightly, but Chris sees it. "Is not end of the world if I have to be starting over."

"I'm not leaving unless you come with me. How else am I going to know which neighborhood to pick?"

Ulie laughs, "Your wife picks for you. Otherwise, you live on the street."

"Tee hee," Chris feigns. Ulie's goofy laughter makes him smile though.

"Because you cannot make decision for yourself," Ulie clarifies. He opens the door to Crosswords letting "Blue Suede Shoes" spill out into the streets.

"I got it," Chris laughs. "You staying down here a while?"

"Davai!" Ulie, already bouncing on his long legs, folds the description and slides it into his pocket. "Blue Suede Shoes" has become Ulie's favorite song in recent days. He pulls on the collar of his polo, but his friendship with Chris has taught him that removing his shirt is not as accepted as it perhaps once was. But he does untuck the orange and white striped polo from his blue jeans and kicks into some arhythmic jerks and swings Chris takes for dancing. The other patrons give him plenty of space, and a roar of excitement rises to the ceiling with raised bottles. It's overwhelming how quickly things have changed. Ulie has gone from the subject of gossip traded in whispers behind the backs of hands, to a Russian-American Urban legend, a true underdog to king-of-the-hill story. A powerful wave of pride crashes down on Chris.

"Don't drink too much, bud," Chris says. But Ulie is in another world now.

Chris turns to the stairs, catching a glimpse of the waitress at whom Aditi always stares a little too long. He wonders if Aditi will be his neighbor. Heaven's got to be enormous and there are far more people there than alive. The waitress meets his eyes, and the corner of her mouth turns up as she turns away. "Blue Suede Shoes" ends and the band kicks into "Burning Love."

"Lord of Mighty!" Ulie shouts. He tugs on his collar as though his temperature is rising.

Is that the real Elvis? Chris thinks for the umpteenth time.

Chris backs through the swinging door to the stairway. The music follows him all the way up to his apartment. It doesn't die down until he shuts it out behind the apartment door, and even then, he can still feel the kickdrum beat when he pays attention. He drags himself to his room and falls onto his bed. His mind tries to imitate sleep again. He sees Andrea speed walking down the sidewalk trying to find the kid and his mother. Hoping for answers. He jogs after her to the faint voice bouncing to the rhythm of a sprint. "I'm gonna poop my pants!" he hears.

Still no closure.

"Do you think he did it?" Andrea asks. Her voice tumbles around in his mind. She turns back to him with sunken eyes and gray veins crawling up her pale neck.

Chris winces and sits up from the bed. He walks to the living room, forgetting again that Aditi won't be there to talk sports, or make fun of politics, or talk about best or most hilarious ways to die, anything to get his mind off it. He misses her. That blunt force attitude, the ability to always make him laugh with some horrible joke or poke at reality. It had only been a week, but in the entire time Chris called suite 5B of the Crossroads Building his home, Aditi had been there for everything. He leans against her bedroom doorway smelling Ulie's B.O. and chicken strips. It has conquered the familiar smell of beer and perfume that had been there. He's pleased to discover that Aditi's face comes to him with no effort at all. He wonders if this is because of his mind's recency bias or if death is so traumatic that it wiped the memory of his wife's face. He recalls his first date with Andrea. Their wedding day. The day they met. Begging his mind to show her face.

Chris lies on the floor, homing in on the happiest he had ever been. It was vacation. He and Andrea had been to the beaches of Southern California for a week. He remembers lying on the beach under an umbrella. The sun was out, and he could feel her head on his shoulder, could smell her shampoo, that sweet cucumber, flowery aroma that meant she was home. He can smell it now. Waves crashed just a few yards away. The sun was warm on his feet and stomach. The wind picked up, knocking over the umbrella. His face warmed. No, not his face. His head.

The memory changes. Suddenly a numb sensation swells from the center of his forehead. A spot burns into his skull. He sees the sky. Around his vision, there is an overgrowth of grass. He feels someone pulling his feet. He hears a voice from farther away. Chris's eyes spring open, and a weak yelp escapes his throat. His heart thrums in his chest. He touches his forehead and gets only a sheen of sweat.

"I have to get out of here," Chris announces to the empty apartment.

He gets off the floor and walks past the red Naugahyde couch to the kitchen. On the refrigerator, a small magnetic dry erase board clings to the surface. He jots a quick note to Ulie with the dry-erase marker clipped to the side and leaves the apartment.

Chris descends the stairs to the bar to the sounds of "Don't Be Cruel." It's a rowdier rendition than he's ever heard. As he pushes through the swinging door, he sees that Ulie and three other barflies have joined The King and his band on stage. The crowd has nearly doubled, and it takes an uncomfortable couple of minutes to push through them for Chris to get to the door. He gets outside just as the crowd shouts the lyrics back up to the stage. Chris powerwalks around the people on the sidewalk, desperate to get back to the mailbox building. He takes up jogging in the bike lane.

Chris opens the mailroom door to calamity again, tripping over a skateboard. He catches his balance and hurries through the lobby. He rounds the corner reaching for his dial and comes to a stop so quickly that he slips in the puddle of water on the floor rolling on his ankle. The sudden pain causes him to shout, startling the man wearing just a towel and necklace who is shimmying open his mailbox.

"Whoa, you good bro?"

"I'm fine, just slipped," Chris says struggling to his feet.

"I've been there," he bonks himself on the forehead then crosses his eyes and pokes his tongue out the side of his mouth. He awkwardly laughs, watching Chris climb to his feet. "That's why I'm here."

"That was pretty easy to put together on my own." Chris winces and sucks air over the blazing pain in his ankle.

"Hey man, do you need help?"

"No thanks," Chris says. "I'm just checking the mail. I'll go after you."

"Alright," he says. He returns to the dial. "I'm Isaac. Just let me know if I can help." After a few moments, Isaac opens his mailbox. An envelope waits for him. He rips it open and turns to the page with his latest score. A strange moment passes when Chris wonders if Isaac knows how to read. Isaac's hands drop to his side. He shrieks, and Chris flinches away. "Yes! Number two! One more six and I'm out this bitch!"

Chris eases to the mailbox, and dials in the combination. He opens the door, and waiting for him over the sticker from the Guild is a golden envelope. His fingers tremble so badly that the envelope nearly falls to the ground. He opens it, and sitting on top of the feedback document, there is a keycard. The keycard falls into Chris's open hand. He looks down the hall to the golden elevator doors. He runs.

# Chapter 6
## SAY HELLO 2 HEAVEN

Getting into Heaven is almost a religious experience. The elevator is dark, and the speakers play a waltzy six/eight rhythm. Chris can hear the light sizzle of a thin chain dangling onto the ride. Four walls made from a heavy, sturdy wood surround him. He figures mahogany, because it's the only wood he knows that isn't cherry or rosewood or pine. Mirrors are placed so high up the wall that he thinks even Ulie would have difficulty using them. An upright bass thumps along with the quiet swinging beat; a familiar feeling stirs up the urge within Chris to sway back and forth on the toes of his hightops. Filled with a cocktail of jubilation, excitement, anxiety, and numb exhaustion, his head rocks back and forth, chin lifting and falling with the rise and fall of the notes. Then the piano crawls up and down the chords like a familiar guitar riff. He picks up the lyrics as the drummer's fans crash quietly onto the cymbal. His voice will never be Cornell's, but neither will anyone else's. He mumbles the lyrics to "Say Hello 2 Heaven."

The elevator trundles onward, but Chris can't tell if its trajectory is up or down, only that it is moving. He glances down at the panel with the two buttons—the six is dark and the ten is glowing a dull yellow—and can't find any real sign of a direction. He didn't press either button, so there must be something coded into the keycard, which is a relatively simple thing to do, but Chris raises his eyebrows, impressed just the same.

The music takes over again. Chris finds himself giving into the urge and swaying with the music from side to side. Right with the kick drum, left to the snare. The sizzle of the ride cymbal courses through him like electricity. The elevator moves forward into eternity. Left, two, three. Right, two, three. He adds a snap to each down beat. A flash reaches between the doors, lighting Chris's face with a dull yellow that feels like a sunset. Another flash, a little longer, brighter, and warmer. Another four or five flashes peek through the small space between the doors faster each time, and Chris dons the sunglasses from his shirt pocket. He feels himself slowing, not straight up or down but up, forward, and to the right a little. He stops swaying and nervously waits for the doors to separate, letting in the light. A familiar elevator boop interrupts the music. A feminine voice comes from the speakers.

"Please wait as the music syncs with the trajectory of the elevator."

Chris's brow furrows. He is standing on one foot, waiting for the next down beat to hit. His hand waits in the air in snapping position. "What?" He feels the elevator rumble under his feet jerk enough to make Chris flinch, and then become completely still again. He looks around this dark, silent square room. The ten is still dully lit.

"Recalculating."

He doesn't feel movement but there is a flash of light. He hears a voice, very quiet, very muddy, then six taps of the fans on the edge of the snare, one-two-three, one-two-three. The music continues just as the music is building to the chorus. Chris mumbles under his breath about a man who came from an island and died in the street. The music builds to a point where the anticipation is so much Chris couldn't continue singing. The music crescendos and cuts out on a loud snare beat. The elevator doors open, and the titular line fills Chris's mind. The bright blue sky is so overwhelming that he nearly loses his balance. The view is enormous.

He collects himself and steps weakly onto the platform. Below, a long set of concrete stairs lead to an open park. Beyond that a small tree line only a few-dozen-feet-wide opens to a short beach and a brilliant blue ocean. The water so clear that the sand can easily be seen a half mile offshore. He hears something that he hasn't heard in months—maybe over a year, time doesn't really make sense anymore with no sleep—a dog is barking somewhere. Around him there are other elevators connected by the platform at the top of the stairs. He follows the sound of the dogs and realizes that it's coming from behind the elevators where he can't see. The golden elevators are joined by an eight-foot wall of marble.

Each elevator has a railing leading down the steps to a person in black slacks, a white button-up shirt, and a purple and yellow vest. Chris makes his way down the steps, gazing along the lush trees and into the forever beyond that ocean. He is mesmerized by the world unfolding in front of him. There are birds in the air. Everything is so colorful. Even the concrete steps have a kind of beautiful silver hue. Chris raises his sunglasses to wipe his eyes.

"Hello, friend," the man in the vest says. He is around forty and his smile is perfect save for the gap between his front teeth. Chris is welcomed, almost pulled in, by the look on the man's face. He has been bald long enough that he has no tan line. His shirt is pressed, and the vest is clean velvet with a tailor-made fit. His eyes are a bright amber hue that almost looks like colored contacts. "Welcome to Heaven."

"Yeah," Chris says, clearing his throat. "Hell of a view. I was expecting the dogs, but this kind of blew me away."

"Yes, the Guild of Divinity has structured the entrance to Heaven so that it will create the greatest impact. Everything else should be in line with what you expect." He hands Chris a small white box. "This will be your beeper."

"A beeper?" Chris removes the lid of the small box, and under it is, in fact, a small black beeper.

"Yep," he says, happily. "It's a little outdated, but the Guild has stood by the idea that once technology can do what you want it to, it's cumbersome to pile on, you know? Your beeper is how you do pretty much everything in Heaven. You want to find your house, just press the red button, and ask for directions."

"Sure," Chris says. "So, whatever I need, I just press the red button to talk, and then ask for it?"

"That's correct." The man puts his hands together. He leans forward slightly like a bellhop silently asking for a tip. "Now, is there anything else I can answer for you?"

"Is this your job?" Chris asks. "Like, is this what you do for eternity?"

"Until I want to file for a transfer," he says, smiling. "But if you're asking if this is what I chose to do, yes. I love the look on people's faces when they see the ocean. You and those sunglasses made it a difficult one, ya rascal." He laughs like someone in a 1950s sitcom.

Chris draws back in surprise. Smiling, he says, "Just ask this thing where to go?"

"Oh, I apologize. You'll need to touch your keycard to the beeper to turn it on."

"Like this?" Chris touches the keycard to the beeper. There is a familiar boop.

"That's it. Have a great day. Welcome to Heaven!"

Chris walks past him, focused on the impossibly clear sea. He presses the red button.

"Hello, Christopher," a voice says. It was the same voice that recalculated the elevator and music a few minutes before. "Welcome to your first day in Heaven."

"Okay, cool," Chris says. He presses the red button again. "Um, do you know where I live? I have no idea what I'm doing here. Also, it's fine if you just call me Chris."

"Hello, Chris. Yes, I do know where you live. Would you like to go there now? There is an excited little dog named Waffles waiting for you."

"Please," Chris says, much louder than he meant to. "Sorry, yes please, take me there. Also, are you a real person or a robot…er…thing?"

"I am an automated system. But you can set a name to call me. Setting a name for me will allow you to call me without pressing a button."

Chris nods impressed. Just like everything else I talk to.

"Might I suggest, Bilhah. Or Billie if you prefer. To reach your home, please turn to your right and follow the sidewalk around the elevator perron."

Chris does as the beeper says, using the arrow on the screen like a compass. As he rounds the steps, he watches the faces of the people who view the forest and ocean. Like zombies, but in a good way. He can certainly understand why someone would choose to do this. But he puts himself in that position and can't see it making him happy for long.

Chris follows the sidewalk around the elevator perron—whatever that is—and follows it away from the ocean. Behind the elevators, couples and families play with dogs in the rest of the park. Man, the Guild really knows how to make an entrance. The trees in the park are wide and tall. There is ample space between each one, and dogs run in all directions, barking and wrestling. Little fat dogs play with scrawny poodle-haired dogs. A pack of huskies chat in their strange screaming voices to each other. A rogue tennis ball bounces toward Chris, and a golden retriever follows. Chris picks up the slobbery green ball. The dog taps his feet in excitement. After a convincing pump fake, Chris tosses the ball. He hears someone thank him. Chris follows Billie's directions through the dog park.

On the opposite side of the park is a structure that appears to be vending machines crammed into a bus stop. He continues toward it, taking in the smell of soil and the energy of the dogs swirling around like an enjoyable version of the mailbox building in Purgatory Enterprises. At the end of the park, there is a marquee made of iron declaring this the Welcome Home Park. Next to the sign is the bus stop, but the vending machines don't have anything to see beyond the windows. Chris puts his face against the glass but only sees black. Someone snickers behind him. He steps back from the machine, eyeballing it suspiciously. There are two red circles on either side of the screen. He presses the red button on the beeper. "Hey, Billie. What are these vending machine things?"

Billie says, "These are Community Interest Machines—or CIMs—there are many artists, filmmakers, musicians, et cetera, who operate for Purgatory Enterprises. These screens will link to your thumbprints, and as you find more interests, the CIMs will suggest new artists."

"Hang on, we still work for Purgatory Enterprises?"

"There is only Purgatory Enterprises, run by the Guild of Divinity."

Chris can't stop the confused grimace from forming on his face. There will be time to analyze that later he is certain. The Guild will provide. Chris backs away from the vending machine. At the next machine, a tall, skinny kid places each of his thumbs on a red dot. A voice, much like Billie's, greets the kid. The screen displays a loading bar for a moment and then a list. The kid swipes and touches the screen over and over too quickly for Chris to keep up, so he decides to move on. After all, he's not here to watch a stranger touch a screen. He follows the arrow on his beeper.

"You know, I heard your voice over there. You're not cheating on me are you, Billie?"

"I don't understand."

"It was—never mind. Look, I don't see any houses, how far is the walk?"

"Nine point seven three miles."

"Oh." Chris stops on the sidewalk. He looks back to the vending machine that operates with thumbprints and keeps up with personal preferences with touchscreen capabilities. Then he looks at the black square in his hand, this thing that would have him walk for nine point seven miles if he had not asked. Then back to the vending machine that operates with thumbprints and keeps up with personal preferences with touchscreen capabilities. One of the few sentences the man at the entrance said to him comes back to him. The Guild has stood by the idea that once technology can do what you want it to, it's cumbersome to pile on, you know? Then he looks at the black square. "Hey, Billie, can I get a ride there?"

"I have alerted a shuttle. Sam will arrive shortly in a yellow four-door sedan."

"Excuse me, sir," an enthusiastic voice calls to Chris. A man is leaning over the console, peering at him through the passenger window of a yellow four-door sedan. His hair is neatly combed back, and his mustache is extraordinary. He's wearing a white Henley and black jeans. "Are you Christopher?"

"Yeah, just Chris though."

"Hop on in." Sam's voice is somewhere at the intersection of mid-western, southern, and turn-of-the-century flamboyant.

Chris pauses, familiarity tugging on his mind. "Do I know you?"

"No, I don't believe," Sam says, cheerily enough. "I never forget a face. I just got a notification. Says that you need a ride. Where to?"

"I—" Chris looks around for street signs on the sidewalks. People glance at him. Afraid of becoming a spectacle, he climbs into the back seat. "I actually don't know. I'm just trying to get home. But I don't know where that is."

"Oh, you're new?" Sam turns to the back, pointing to a small black circle on the door. "Just touch your beeper to that. And I'll get the address that way."

Chris touches the beeper to the black circle on the door. There's a familiar boop.

"And I've got it," Sam calls to the backseat. The car pulls away from the curb and U-turns. "So, it's your first day? How do you like it so far?"

The car accelerates, bringing the realization that within minutes, Andrea will be back in his life—or him back in hers. A flurry of excitement tickles at Chris. "It was a little overwhelming actually. I teared up. It's all so normal though."

"It's like that at first, I know," Sam says, grinning behind his mustache. "But after the first part, you get used to it very quickly. Have you decided what you want to do? No pressure. You can change it. Change it every day if you want. I've lost count how many times I've been transferred. I love adventure. There's no reason not to just set off and explore. You have so much time now."

Chris squints, and his head tilts in thought. "Yeah...I actually don't know. I just want to see my wife. She'll help. Hell, I may actually just be a comedian and tell stories until I figure it out."

"I do like humor. Are you a storyteller?" Sam sniffs. The push broom under his nose wiggles.

"Not yet," Chris says. He looks out the window, watching the buildings pass. There's a football stadium down a collection of streets with people flocking toward it. He's eager to see the baseball park. Hopefully, the Heaven team is good this season. Chris has always been a homer. "I have stories to tell though."

"Oh, yeah," Sam says. "I understand that. Where were you from?"

"Chicago." Chris finds the question slightly off, but completely accurate.

"Smalltown in Missouri, myself. Baseball fan?"

"Big time," Chris says, working the word 'Missouri' over in his head.

"Baseball park is right down the street from your neighborhood. You can probably hear it from your back yard. If it's a close one anyway."

Chris watches the buildings become shorter as the drive continues to his home. People line the sidewalks, walking to restaurants, outdoor shops, and even a multiplex theater. There are dogs on leashes. People wearing jerseys of teams he's never heard of. They pass an enormous fountain under which a collection of children and parents splash each other. He's confident that he'll be able to find anything he needs at any time of day or night. Trees spring up along the street. Eventually the sidewalk thins, and the people become sparser. Sam slows the car for a turn. Outside the window the city becomes a neighborhood with roundabouts, cul-de-sacs, and even picket fences. There's a navy-blue house with white trim. A brick, two-story house with an open garage. A motorcycle is propped up inside, its paint glimmering in the daylight. A man is mowing the front lawn of a lime green duplex. Then Sam stops the car at a sidewalk leading up to a wooden house with chocolate colored trim, a carport, and a bright red door. Chris pulls his sunglasses off and stuffs them back into his shirt pocket. This was their home. It's not in their neighborhood but definitely their home. Waffles bounces at the narrow windows flanking the door. Her happy little brown face is smiling. She has already smeared nose prints on two of the rectangular panes. Chris can't move. His fingers tremble and drop Billie into the floorboard. He scrambles to pick it up.

"It's okay, friend," Sam says. His voice is low and he's watching the world outside the windshield. "The worst part is over. You've already died. What else is going to happen to you? Want some advice?" Chris doesn't—can't—speak. "Remember this feeling. Right before your life starts. Last time it will happen."

"Can I ask you something?" Chris says softly. His eyes never leave Waffles.

"You can." Sam leans forward, resting his arms on the steering wheel.

"Are you Mark Twain?"

Sam laughs. It's a jolly laugh. "Don't you think you've waited long enough?"

Chris opens the door of the yellow sedan. Waffles's muffled barks come to him across the yard. The trauma of watching cancer kill his wife, the trauma of dying, the trauma of not being able to turn his mind off for months. It all intertwines, wraps itself around Chris, knocking him to his knees.

One step at a time, he tells himself, climbing to his feet. He doesn't know why he does it, perhaps to save himself a trip, but he checks the mailbox before starting for the front door. Inside is a single-sided, light-blue card with the Guild of Divinity's masthead, and below that are two lines of text written in ink so black that light won't reflect off it. The first asks for his name. And the second stiffens Chris's chest with anxious helplessness. A single word asking, "Occupation: _____."

He slides the card in his back pocket, knowing the time has come to decide, and follows the muffled barks across the yard.

Waffles's legs bounce the chunky body up and down with each yip. A black circle sits in place of the knob on the door. He places Billie on the circle and hears a click. He pushes the door open, and Waffle barrels forward. The dog whimpers with uncontrollable glee, wiggling her thick pit bull body like a fish. Chris bends his knees and Waffles leaps into his arms. The two roll onto the floor of the foyer. Slobber flies, and Chris delivers smooches and pets. It turns to playful wrestling. "Choo wanna go ou'side?!" Chris says. Waffles freezes, eyes wild. Her big feet stomp down, ready to pounce. "'ets go!"

The foyer Ts after a few feet. To the left there are bedrooms, and to the right there is a living room, kitchen, and dining room. French doors in the living room let out to the fenced-in backyard. Waffles bolts through the living room to the back door. She jumps at the doorknob. Once, twice, three times, as if to say, "hurryhurryhurryhurryhurry!"

"Okay, Okay!" Chris opens the door, and Waffles flies into the yard with the ultimate euphoric exuberance. He closes the door, unable to hide his smile. "Hun?" Chris calls into the house. The leather couch in the living room points at a television. He wonders what new channels they'll get. There's a small pink chair from his mother's house sitting below the opening in the wall between the kitchen and living room. He leans around the wall to the kitchen. The cabinets are closed—which only means Chris hasn't been in there to leave them open—and the pots and pans dangle from the fixture over the island prep table. Andrea's rooster hand towel straddles the sink faucet. There's a familiar light blue card on the dining room table. Give me a minute, would ya? "Hun, are you home?" Chris turns away from the kitchen to the bedroom, banging his foot on the glass coffee table as he has done so many times it hardly hurts anymore. Waffles's bed lies between it and the couch. No one has moved a thing. The movie posters from his and Andrea's first four dates hang in the hallway. No one is in the guest bathroom on the left. The guest bedroom is closed as always. The master is open, he can see the edge of the bed come into view; the red and purple striped comforter lies wrinkle-free in its place. Then the open bathroom door, glazed shower door closed. From what he can see, it stands empty. "Hun?"

He comes into the room, no one on the bed. No one in the bathroom. There is only a sheet of paper waiting on the dresser. There is something vital missing from this house. The flowery smell of shampoo. He lifts the piece of paper and gets no further than, "I'm sorry," in Andrea's handwriting, before his legs give, and he collapses onto the floor.

# Chapter 7
## IT'S FINE

A knock on the front door from someone outside the blankness behind his eyelids. It's still ajar from Chris's arrival, and Aditi's voice rings through the house. "Hello? It's me, Aditi. We lived together at the Crossroads Building." The creaky door opens slowly. She walks to where the hallway Ts. "I'm announcing myself, so you don't freak out when—what the fuck!" Aditi runs to Chris. She kneels beside him, calling his name and lightly slapping his cheeks.

"Stop it."

"Why are you wet?" Aditi demands. Chris hands her the piece of paper. She reads the full letter, learning more than Chris has. It's a litany of cliches from "I just need to be my own person" to "You need someone who makes you happy." Chris's eyes stay closed, afraid that the moment they open he'll see Aditi rolling her eyes and making vomiting gestures. She exhales deeply. "Do you really need a whole page to say fuck all? What's this bullshit about being the sun in someone else's sky?"

"It's a Pearl Jam lyric."

"Ugh! What a cunt," she says, unable to hide the face she's making. When he doesn't laugh at the word he always laughs at, she deflates. "I'm sorry, Chris. I should've known when I didn't see anyone. Waffles wasn't even here until this morning."

Chris is silent, covering his face with his hands. His body is numb.

"You're wearing so many bracelets." Aditi stands and pulls his hands away from his face, "Come here…come here. Come here." Chris can't move even with what he feels is a genuine attempt at leaning up. Aditi grabs him by the shoulders and drags him down the hall to the living room. She props him up at the front of the couch next to Waffles's bed. Aditi paces from side to side of the living room, pulling her hair into a loose ponytail. "I can do two things for this. One, I'm going to try to make you laugh in a way only I can. And two, I'm going to make you uncomfortable in a way that only I can…I'll take your silence to mean that I should proceed. I live across the street by the way. I had them give me a house close by so some jagoff wouldn't have to deal with…this." She gestures at her feet toward Chris, who is looking to somewhere beyond the floor. "We have a neighbor who was a bit of a partier. The way he died was at a Buffalo Bills tailgate all the way in Kansas. They were jumping through a flaming table in a Circuit City parking lot. He, mentally tossed like a salad, using a bottle of lighter fluid and a taser to make flame gun, catches his face on fire. Everyone starts throwing beer on him, which in the frozen air freezes on his body. He's running around in circles looking for a patch of snow, in a parking lot. He can't find one, because someone has cleared the parking lot so eventually, he bites it, but the best part is—here it is—that he falls on the taser. Under his weight, the taser goes off and for just a brief second…it jolts him back to life."

Chris blinks.

"Okay, plan B." Aditi turns on the television, and reaches into her pocket. "Billie, can you play 'Higher & Higher' on this TV. Jackie Wilson, please. Not the creepy slowed down pop version by that whiny girl that's making the rounds."

A familiar boop from the television. Next comes a bass riff that leads to some hand percussion. Aditi moves in a much more elegant, flowing way than anyone else. Even at Crossroads she was the best dancer in the room. Her body is like a river wrapped in jeans and a basketball jersey. Her hair flies back and forth. Her shoulders dip and shake. When the guitar comes in, she mimes the rhythm on her air guitar and shimmies closer to him. She takes his hands from his eyes and lifts his chin. "Your love," she mouths. She points to the roof as the words continue, hips rocking back and forth. Her feet slide forward and backward to the rhythm. The chorus comes and Aditi mouths the lyrics. "Where're my backup singers?"

Chris's gaze falls back to the floor.

"Liftin me!" she shouts, heaving Chris's slender frame to his feet.

He stands there, a sad mannequin. Aditi dances around the living room. A second verse comes. "Come on. I look stupid doing this by myself." In the background of the song, trumpets play and Chris, remembering only a passable amount of trumpet, puts his thumb to his lips and juts the pinkie in the opposite direction. He watches the ground and uses the middle fingers on one hand to play the fingers on the other like the valves on a trumpet.

"That's the shit!" Aditi says, a grin stretching across her face. "Billie, turn it up! Take me to the chorus!" She mouths the words.

Chris mouths the backing vocals. His lips quiver. His feet, knees, waist, and shoulders are all planted firmly where she left them. But she dances around him tossing tissues from a box on the coffee table like confetti.

"Yes!" She shouts. They continue through the chorus, Aditi shimmying up to him. She puts her arm around him and rocks with him, bouncing much more than he will allow for himself. She continues to dance around the room, and when the chorus ends, she switches from air guitar to air trombone to really bring out the brass section. Outside, Waffles yips with excitement. They dance around the room through the third verse. Their eyes meet. Chris steps toward her, and his legs fold. Aditi catches him on the way to the floor. She hugs him tightly, hearing his sobs. "It's fine," she whispers.

"What am I going to do?" he asks.

Aditi doesn't say anything for a long time. "Baby steps. First, you need to go tell that giant baby where you are. He just got his second ten. Everyone here is talking about him. But really, it's because of you. Really, it's you and me. I was there too, but really, it's you. Even if all you do is tell him where you are and wish him luck. You can't just bail on your friend. You only get one time to go back and get anything you left. Take a minute to collect yourself. Then go." She holds him at arm's length. "Shit, you look horrible."

# Chapter 8
## JESUS

Chris stands outside Crossroads at the Scare Board, looking up to the top row, second client from the right. His eyes are red and puffy, fingers fidgeting with the hem of his shirt. He reaches for the yellowing slip of paper but stops to peer around. The focus seems to be on a fire breather and accordion player. He snatches the paper from the tack. He pushes through the front door to an Elvis song he doesn't recognize. Or maybe he does, but his mind is on the description. He's reading every last word on the piece of paper as he crosses the bar to the stairway and up to 5E. His legs carry him around the clusters of people scattered through the hallways and around his door. As if with muscle memory, his hand opens the door to his old apartment. It's quiet. He looks up to see the empty red couch, and the door to Ulie's room ajar. He pushes through to his bedroom. The description falls into the tray as Chris falls into the chair. His eyes close, and gravity moves underneath his feet. His equilibrium shifts. His weight transfers from his seat to his high-tops. He holds out his hand, and he feels the cold steel bar of the prison cell door.

  A single fingernail ticks the seconds off on a steel bar. tik tik tik. The sound rolls through the G-Block corridor of the Colline County Penitentiary like the ripples from a drop of water. Chris stands facing the hallway from inside the fourth cell. Dead center of the corridor. The sodium lights give the corridor a muddy orange light that falls on the cold concrete walls and floors. If Chris didn't already know, he would be certain that sound was the tiny gears of a clock ticking into eternity. He turns his attention to the cell where a man sits cross legged reading a leather-bound book. Voices murmur, rising and falling all around him like waves on the shore, or wind through tall grass.

"Come on, Jesus," Chris says. His voice doesn't bounce from wall to wall like everyone else's. It ignores the cinderblock walls completely and pierces straight into Jesus's heart. "You really want that to be the last thing you ever read?"

"My name isn't Jesus," he says. His eyes remain on the thin, leather bound pages. "It's Jesús."

"Okay," Chris laughs. Never mind that he was Jesus until he went to prison or that his real name is Tyler, and Jesus was just a high school nickname because of his hair. Chris runs his hand across the bars. He feels each bar beneath his fingers, but there's no sound. It's a sensation he never truly grasped. Even touch has a sound in this kind of quiet. He hears the tik tik tik of the fingernail. "I'm just saying, it's fine if you're looking for salvation in a last-ditch effort to right your wrongs. But you're in the front of that book. Those parts are just going to bum you out. You'll want to skip to the back of the book if you're looking for inspiration."

"Leave me alone."

"I can't really say anything, I guess. The last one I read was The Pelican Brief." Chris wraps his fingers around the bars and pulls with all his strength. He isn't surprised when nothing happens. The sodium light from the hallway washes into the cell. There's not a more troubling reminder that Chris is dead like not having a shadow. The toilet is on one side of the room, and the bed is on the other. Jesus sits on the floor in the darkness of the G-block of the penitentiary. "Kind of a shithole, isn't it? I guess there's no reason to spend a lot of money on a building people don't leave."

Jesus closes the book and lays it on his lap.

"Well, this is it," Chris says. "Your last bedroom."

Jesus's head falls into his open, shaking hands.

"You know what they say about people about to 'ride the lightning,'" Chris chuckles. Jesus didn't answer. "A special kind of adrenaline kicks in. It affects people differently, but there's a general checklist. Makes you numb. Shake. Some people lock up and can't move. Some find an inhuman strength and try to fight their way out. Some, like you, even hallucinate." Chris stops. He tries to make eye contact with Jesus, but his face remains covered by beaten and scarred hands. The knuckles are swollen from dislocations and breaks in fights during his life, both in and out and now back in prison. "It'll be over in the blink of an eye."

"Just let them kill me," Jesus says. His voice weakly spreads through the room.

"That's a bit dramatic. Are you telling me that you don't deserve this?"

Jesus drops his hands. He stares at them blankly.

"Look at me," Chris said. Jesus doesn't move. His eyes freeze, trained on the stained concrete floor beyond his hands. "You never have seen me as a person, have you? That's how you get around feeling remorse for what you do to people, right? You don't think of them as people." Chris waits for a response. When he is convinced that nothing would come, he asks, "What did you think of me when you killed me?"

"Just shut up!" Jesus hisses. He lunges toward Chris. His mangled hands reach for a neck that wasn't there. Jesus opens his eyes. He is at the cell door gripping the bars.

"Warden!" the inmate known as "Clocks" shouts from the cell next to Jesus's. "Warden! He's losin' his marbles. Better come plug him in now 'fore he makes a mess a'hisself!"

"Fuck you, Clocks. I'm having a bad dream."

"Dream? What you sleepin' for over'ere? Devil's waitin' on you! He'll get you in your dreams." Clocks cackles.

The corridor roars to life. The other inmates in the G-block shout verbal threats at Jesus and Clocks. Chris lets the cacophony blast through the room without saying anything. He moves to the corner of the cell, sliding down the wall as his legs lose strength. A flash of sky surrounded by overgrown grass. He rubs at the warm spot on his forehead. He wants to picture Andrea, but even if he could remember her face, he's lost the joy it brings him. It's just a habit he hasn't started to break yet. The feeling of disconnecting from his limbs, one by one, cripples him. He thinks of Aditi instead.

A heavy metal door opens. A white light brightens the block. A shadow pours down the concrete corridor. "Shut up or I'm bringing the keys!" The roar continues for one last word, then quickly silences.

"Whatchoo gonna do?" Clocks says.

The shadow withdraws. The sound of keys jingling and two

bodies return. Guards dressed in navy uniforms storm past the cell. The keys jingle in the locks, and the beating begins. It starts with shouts, then progresses past groans and whimpers to pleas. After what feels like hours later, it ends in silence. The guards lock the cell. The door closes, banishing the white light. And the block burns to dull again.

Chris wipes his face, summons the strength to stand. A moment later, the tik tik tik of the fingernail on metal continues. What am I doing? he asks himself. Jesus stands up and moves to the plastic mattress. He hangs his head, not looking at Chris the entire time. But Chris watches him. "Do you even remember me?"

"Leave me alone," Jesus says.

"I was visiting my parents in Florida." Chris says. "They live in the woods, right? So, to really get a good cell phone signal, you have to walk either a quarter mile toward the interstate, or about a half a mile behind their house to a sugarcane field. Now I was someone who had recently fallen face first into a runner's lifestyle, I was willing to get the extra steps. I ran angry, too. Like I wasn't even running. Just stomping on the ground."

"Just leave me—"

"Good people die slowly all the time," Chris snaps. "What makes you think that after everything you've done, you get to speed this up?"

"I haven't done anything to you." Jesus turns his eyes to the high window.

Chris's jaw clinches so hard that for a moment he thinks it's locked. "You're a liar. You've always been, and you've believed every single lie you've ever told."

"Bullshit," Jesus says under his breath.

"You told people you were the drummer for Mazzy Star." Chris ticks that off on a finger. Jesus scoffs and pushes further from the edge of the bed. "Oh, so you were? Humor me then. Play 'Fade Into You.' Should be easy. It's the one song everyone knows by Mazzy Star."

Jesus says, "I don't have my kit."

"Play your lap. Real drummers slap their thighs and stomp their feet."

Jesus looks at Chris's feet. "Fine." Jesus plays eight beats of a less than basic drum riff.

Chris interrupts. "I said 'Fade Into You'."

"That's what I played."

"What you played was four/four time. 'Fade Into You' is six/eight. The drummer for Mazzy Star would know that. Do you even know who Mazzy Star is, or are they just popular enough for no one to call you on your bullshit?"

"What, you come here to call me out on a lie I told people twenty years ago?"

"No, I'm here to make you understand that what you did, you did to another human being. Someone with a life and problems of his own." Chris leans forward to force eye contact, but Jesus's view remains out the window. "You also stole from people. Money out of your mom's purse. Watches from friends. Jewelry. An antique motorcycle once and traded it for dope."

"Get out of my face with that shit."

"Then you sold the dope and blew the money on meth."

"Shut your fuckin' mouth."

"Or what, you'll look me in the eye?" Chris leans forward again. "You're here for a reason. Who else did you kill, Jesús?"

"I ain't killed nobody, man!" He shouts, his voice echoing around the walls.

"I ain't kilt nobody neither!" a clear, mocking voice cackles from the darkness among the others. "But I put the yolk on your momma though. I make the soup. You know, I make the soup!"

The heavy metal door bangs open again. The white sheet of light falls on the corridor. A silhouette stands in the doorway like a living eclipse. Everyone forfeits their last words in favor of a painless night's sleep.

tik tik tik

Nothing. The suffocating weight of the silence fills the room like a fog. The metal door slams, taking the light and the shadow.

"Then why are you here?" Chris says.

"Wrong place, wrong time."

"You're a liar."

"My mom ain't raise a liar."

"She raised a murderer."

Jesus springs off the bed. A look of horror stretches his face open as he meets Chris's eyes for the first time.

"What?" Chris says. He steels himself against the incredible urge to break eye contact. Being this close makes his skin crawl. "Smell the ditch that you left me in?"

"I don't know you," Jesus turns away. "You just some guy someone shot."

"You're not wrong," Chris says, moving forward. "But you're not a liar, are you? Not a thief either? Certainly, never killed anybody."

"None of it," Jesus drops on the plastic bed, covering his face with his hands.

"Who was the drummer of Mazzy Star?"

"Go away, dude," Jesus pleads.

"Why was there a black 1975 Harley Sportster in your garage for a month and three weeks?" Chris asks. He can feel the anger and embarrassment boiling. He holds his place at the foot of the bed, defiantly. "Were you just holding that for a friend?"

"Bro, I don't even—"

"Who killed Christopher Anderson?"

"I don't know," Jesus growls.

One of the inmates rattles the door to his cell. "What don't you know, boy?"

"Who shot me, Jesús?" No answer. "Who left me in a ditch? Alone. Look at me."

"I shot you, okay?" Jesus whispers. "I thought you was a cop. Nobody walks out in that field. Not for no reason…you good now?"

Chris steps back. Everyone wants to believe they lived and died for a purpose. Nobody wants to know that their life ended because of a mistake, let alone a mistake that could've been avoided with a simple maneuver in the opposite direction. More troubling than hearing that his death didn't matter is the fact that knowing it doesn't change how he feels. It just opens the door to his emptiness. Forces him to look at it. And what he sees doesn't scare him. It just makes him furious. He falls against the wall again and watches the ceiling.

"What are you, some kind of ghost?"

"I'm a grim reaper. A skeleton in a cloak."

"You're going to kill me?" A tone of panic comes out of Jesus's mouth.

"No," Chris groans.

"Then what are you even doing here?"

"Because I don't know how to cope with," he stops before he can say that he can't cope with the fact that his wife left him for Hell in a note. "With the fact that I'm dead. That I died alone. Because someone was afraid of being caught breaking the law. The fact that my life was so unimportant to you that you left me in a ditch. My life mattered nothing to you, except it meant confronting what you were doing."

Jesus rediscovers the floor.

They sit in the silence. Chris doesn't know what he really wanted from this, but knowing Jesus recognizes what he's done doesn't give him any relief.

"Jesus—Jesús, I mean—every time I had to make a major decision, I made it too late or the wrong one or someone else made it for me. I blamed myself for the death of my wife. I didn't want to live without her, and I couldn't decide what to do about that. And you're just another person that decided for me." He pauses, finally able to admit to himself that he relied too much on Andrea in his life. And death. He never so much as picked a place to eat dinner. He never tried to move up in his job, because she never asked him to do it. He never learned anything he didn't have to, never went anywhere, or even did anything important, unless she had something do with it. He lost his identity. Everything he was—and is—was wrapped up in her. Just a part of who she was, like a braid in a new haircut. He looks over to Jesus, who is watching him intently. "I'm supposed to scare you. Make you start thinking about other people. How you affect them. But what is that going to do for you now? Whatever's left of your life…" Chris knows that what he wants to say won't help either of them. So, he doesn't. Instead, he does what he's supposed to do. "You need to think about what you did to other people. There's your starting point, bud. Think of all the good you extinguished in the world by adding evil to it. I'll save you some time. That book your reading? The point is to be a good person to other people."

Chris feels the gravity sliding from his shoes to his seat.

"That's what all those books mean."

Chris opens his eyes to his old bedroom. Ulie's voice comes to him from the living room. He doesn't understand the words, but it has the tone of a question. "Privet, kto tam?"

"Ulie? You haven't gone yet, have you? Don't want to miss your third ten."

"My friend! I just get up from the chair," Ulie says.

"Shit, bud. I'm sorry." Chris says.

"Is okay," Ulie says, grinning his crooked smile. "I told her she was not alone."

"I hope you didn't start that way," Chris says.

"I—" Ulie stops, thinking. "I do not know. Where have you been?"

"I'm on the chopping block, baby," Chris says. It isn't a rebel yell but fuck, it feels like one. Ulie's toothy grin squelches the idea that telling him would make him sad, the way he felt when Aditi told him he now admits to himself.

"No way, buddy! Otlichnye novosti! Very awesome!" He squeezes Chris hard enough to crack his back. "I wish I could be there when you get the envelope."

"Don't worry," Chris says, his spine popping like bubble wrap. "I'll be waiting for you when you get yours."

# Chapter 9
## THE GUILD OF DIVINITY

Chris and Aditi drink shots at the bar every time a player makes a three-point shot on the muted television above the bar. Chris is using the light blue card with the black ink as a coaster. A tinny pop song fills the air with ambience. He can no longer remember what the name of the bar is, but there's a nice breeze coming through the open patio area, and he doesn't care. It's a game from Heaven's minor league between the Bruins and the Apostles, but the majors are still in training camp. Got to start somewhere. The bar seems to be pulling heavily for the Apostles, but Chris grew up a Cubs and Bears fan. That's not something a person shakes just because they die, and if too many more threes come through, it's going to be difficult to hide it. Chris's and Aditi's giggling comes to a quick halt.

"Uh oh," Aditi says, gesturing toward the entrance. Her face creases with concern.

Two men walk into the bar wearing white suits and perfectly styled hair. They walk in lockstep with one another with identical creepy smiles that make their eyes look mismatched. They stop next to Chris. "Christopher Anderson?"

"No 'T'," Chris says, wobbling to his feet. He and Aditi giggle like children.

"The Guild of Divinity has asked to speak to you."

"They not do mailboxes here?" Aditi slurs, and for some reason Chris laughs.

"Yeah, man, put the flag up."

"It's a more urgent matter than a typical mail correspondence."

Chris scoffs. "Okay?"

"Alright," Aditi stands. "Let's go."

"I apologize for the confusion," one of the men holds a hand up to stop her, not dropping his smile. "The Guild has only asked for Mr. Anderson."

"What the f—fuckin' hell is this?" Aditi sits back down. She takes a drink, coughs, and turns back to Chris and the two men. Her eyes stretch open. "Oh, shit. Are they here for me?"

"I gotta go," Chris says to Aditi like a kid leaving the party early. The two men grab him, wrinkling his t-shirt. One of the men swipes the dripping card off the table "I just got out of those other clothes. I'm coming with you, just let me walk."

Only one releases his grip and only to open the door to the back of the bar.

"Are we allowed to go back here?" In the back of the bar are boxes and boxes of liquor that appear to have no beginning or end. The floor is red tile and slightly sticky. Suction sounds with each step. They push through a swinging door, to a small five by ten room with an elevator door. "They keep these everywhere, huh?"

A familiar boop and the doors separate. In the elevator, a jazzy version of "In-A-Gadda-Da-Vida" plays through the speakers. Chris bobs his head. He produces an ornate, metal Pearl Jam lighter from his pocket. He flips open the lid and ignites it.

"Stop," the man still holding his sleeve snaps. He closes the lighter.

"You're drunk, bud," Chris says, holding his hands over his head. He waves them in unison back down to his waist to the beat of the music. The elevator trundles to some destination in the darkness. "I'm hot, guys." He tries to take off his shirt. "Let go, for real." The man gripping his sleeve doesn't loosen. "Where am I going to go?" This question brings no further change. Chris pulls the chest of his shirt and fans himself. Light flashes through the door of the dimly lit elevator. "Does that mean it's going up or down? Feels like we're going…that way." Chris strikes a pose that looks like Elvis Presley, pointing roughly to the high front left corner of the elevator. The lights flash faster and faster. "Oh, I know what that means." Chris mimes a drumroll that begins quickly, but as he loses breath, the noise sputters into silence with his hands by his side, looking at the ceiling. He burps and winces at the burn.

The doors open to a bright white room. Chris holds his hands up to block the light, but it doesn't come from any specific place. It descends on him from everywhere. He feels the hand relinquish his shirt sleeve. "Now, really?"

"Go," the voice behind him demands.

"Where?" Chris says, a dull, sarcastic look on his face.

"Into the room," the other man in the suit says.

Chris whirls around. "No shit?" The men are no longer smiling, something he's never seen from the men in the white suits. Instinctively, Chris stops smiling and stretches to his full height. His face becomes grave, and he backs out of the elevator.

In the room the whiteness pours like an ocean into infinity. Before him, there is a long table. It's not a desk or dais, nothing so spectacular, but a plain white table. There are about a dozen people, evenly split between the men and women, none of whom seem to notice Chris, on the opposite side of the table. The women have hair to their jaw line or longer, most much longer. There's a woman with an afro parted above her right temple. It reaches up like a tidal wave. All the men, two of them completely bald, display random acts of facial hair from unfinished goatees to full lumberjack beards.

Everyone in this room is wearing a navy suit. Chris can see their feet, where the shoes are all different styles and colors. Most of the ones who are sitting cross their legs, either at the ankle or one knee over the other. One of the men, who seems to be taking notes, bounces his leg in quick, irregular intervals. In the middle of the table there is a very tall, strong woman leaning on the table looking at some papers. Her hair is jet black and stops abruptly at her chin. Her skin is pale with dark eyeshadow and bright red lipstick. The man next to her sees Chris and neatly stacks the papers in front of her. All the legs uncross and come together in a neat, business-like seated position. The man taking notes continues to take notes, and his leg continues to bounce. The few of them who were standing take a seat, six on each side of the woman in the middle.

"Mr. Anderson," the tall woman says. "Please, have a seat."

Chris looks around the white space. "There's no chair."

"Oh," she says, finally looking up to him. "Do you mind standing then?"

"Sure," Chris says. His equilibrium seesaws, and he decides to sit anyway.

"My name is Tina," she says, standing to her full height looking down at him. She stands confidently, like a commander. Her voice is low, and in his current state of mind, Chris worries that she might lull him to sleep. "Do you know why we brought you here?"

"Not really," Chris says, searching their faces for clues. "Not my birthday, is it?"

The room—if that's what this place can be called—falls aggressively silent. Tina says, "No. You're here, because you took a client after your time in Purgatory, which itself is against the rules. You didn't perform a task assigned by the description, also against the rules. Instead, you used your place in the afterlife to confront your murderer."

"Surely, that's fine," Chris says, looking at Tina's shoes. The heel is at least three inches high, and there's a small bow the size of a quarter on one, but not the other.

"It's not." Then the woman with white hair two chairs to the left of Tina scoffs. Tina glares over. Somehow the weight of the silence doubles. "Mr. Anderson."

"Chris, please."

"Chris," Tina restarts. "What you've done is very serious. We won't allow people to use the descriptions as a way of exacting some posthumous revenge. Then we'd have people crowding the Scare Boards for personal gain with no consequences."

"To be fair," Chris said. He closes his suddenly heavy eyelids. He crosses his legs and rests his elbows in his lap. "No one cares about the Scare Boards. They don't count, so chauffeurs have no reason to do them. Besides, the one I took was on the board since I got here. No one's in a rush to take a description in their free time."

One of the unnamed faces at the end of the table quietly scratches something, Chris assumes a reminder to look into the Scare Boards, on the top sheet of a notepad.

"It's more than that, Chris," Tina says. "You're not a chauffeur anymore. You could be removed. The rules are different now. You are supposed to know better."

Under her breath, the woman with white hair two chairs to the left of Tina says, "It's not too late." And something else that a more sober Chris may have heard.

Tina snaps, "Judith, you do this every fucking time! If you had a problem with what we all decided was the fair punishment to carry out, you should have said something before now."

"Just continue," Judith says.

"You always undermine everything I do," Tina slams her fist on the table. The man to the right of Tina stands and tries to bring her back to the moment. "No, Marcus. When it's her turn she can do what she wants, but I'm in the middle this time." Judith stands up and shrieks something unintelligible at Tina. The other members of the Guild join the argument, either with shrieks or by breaking off into side groups to gossip about the others. Tina glares down at the stack of papers on the table.

"Can we get through one of these hearings without you making it about yourself, Judith?" Marcus shouts, emphasizing the words with a single upturned finger.

"Oh, my G.O.D.!" Chris shouts. He grabs his temples as if the impending hangover has arrived early. "Do I need to be here for this? I was in my cups, and I would like to return to them."

The Guild freezes. The air thickens. Tina snaps, a sharp sound that echoes like a gunshot. Her face flashes with anger as she marches around the table. "Remove him."

Chris feels hands on both of his shoulders. In that moment he becomes fully sober. One of the men in white suits pins his arms behind him, and that feeling, being too close to a stranger, having no control over what is about to happen, sends a stinging bolt of panic through him. Fear immobilizes him. The other man in a suit flashes a light in his face. Chris feels something even more horrible. Broiling heat, ripping into the scar on his forehead. The pain is nothing he has experienced, and his body locks like he's being electrocuted. He tries to scream, but everything has become white hot pain.

"The problem we have isn't that you took a client after you moved on," Tina says from somewhere beyond the light, and the pain. "It's that you abandoned your friend. You left him to fend for himself because of your own selfish agenda. It doesn't matter that he could handle it."

Chris bites down so hard he thinks his teeth are shifting in the gums. The man readjusts the thing making the light, and Chris sees the smile on his face. The dead-eyed empty grin of a robot. This is something worse than pain, worse than death. For the first time since Andrea's death, Chris doesn't want to die. He just wants this to stop. He wants to survive it. "Wait..."

"You haven't even chosen what you want to do with yourself,"

Tina continues. "You could literally be anything and instead you choose to let other people make decisions for you."

"Please," Chris says, spit flying. The pain is inside his skull. His body fills with the heat. "I'll do anything."

"You won't!" Tina shouts. Her voice is so strong, so intense, that behind her the other people at the table subtly cower away. Her breath burns Chris's already blazing cheeks. He can feel it killing the skin there.

"Let me work for you," he screams, hardly aware that he is the one saying it. This is some kind of safe word, because the heat stops proliferating. His breath comes out jerky and weak as he cultivates the idea. Finally, it comes like a beacon. "Yes. I'll work for you. Let me train the new chauffeurs."

Tina snaps again. The light dies and the pain, or the sudden absence of it, disorients him. The two men in white coats release Chris, and he stumbles back to the floor. Marcus hands Tina a stack of papers, looking over them as she coolly walks around the table to her seat. When she sits back down, she thumbs through the stack, checking the backs of the pages. She lays the papers down on the desk. "These people are your clients. You realize finalized stacks of descriptions are usually twice this thick by the time someone gets to Heaven?" Tina waits. "I guess you're not going to get it."

"I'm drunk again." Chris wobbles at the sudden re-inebriation.

"I know," Tina says, exhausted. "The only reason you still exist is because you are good at what you do. You don't even like being close to people, yet you somehow manage to connect with them." She stares down at the papers in thought. "I think you may be onto something." She slides a separate page across the table. Chris cranes his neck above the table. "Just pick it up." He crawls to the table, wobbly. "This is Ulie's final ten. He didn't have a chance until you showed up, and he has three tens in a row after a week. I will allow you to help people move on to their next place."

Chris tries to clear his vision. He closes his left eye and holds the paper a little further away. "This is only a nine point two," Chris says, looking up from Ulie's score.

"It's a nine point five," Tina says with a damning glare. "We make the rules. We can bend them. Unless you want to tell Ulie he has to start over again. Otherwise, we'll let you deliver the good news, throw a party if you like—take Elvis with you, he'll be happy to entertain."

"That's the real Elvis?"

"Why would we need impersonators?"

Chris shrugs.

Tina holds her palm to him. She shakes her head angrily. When the room is silent, she continues. "We're going to use your skills to move people along. Clear out some space." She nods to the men at the elevator door.

"Clear out some space?"

"Yes. We need to remodel some of the orientation buildings, so we must get these people through as quickly as we can to avoid overcrowding. You have a way of connecting to people like not many people can. You know what it means to have compassion. If you can teach it to other people, then we won't have to remove you. You can take our longest residents under your wing like you did with Ulie."

"Why don't you do it?" Chris asks, not really knowing why he's asking.

"We are the Guild of Divinity," Tina said, defensively. The faces on the rest of the Guild become similarly horrified. The man taking notes finally looks up. Then Tina makes a clear effort to calm herself. As does everyone else in the room. "Yes, that's vague and mysterious, but that's how it works. We can't just step in and do stuff for you. We'll help you, but you've got to help yourself too. It's not supposed to be so difficult. Just show compassion. Do you know why we don't allow chauffeurs to do those three things? Because those things get you out of having to put yourself in the client's position. It exempts you from connection and empathy. It does nothing for the client to know how they die. They can't do anything by the time you get there, anyway. But it makes you think about them. Their fears. Their pain. All we've ever wanted is for people to understand what another person feels. Or at least that another person feels. It shouldn't be that hard. Just don't be a dick." Chris and half the people at the table glare at Judith who is looking at the screen of her Billie. "Since you seem to understand that better than anyone, and while you decide on what you actually want to do forever, we're happy to have you work for us." Chris starts to protest again. She lifts a finger. "Until, of course, you want to file for transfer."

"So, you need me, is that right?"

"Sure," Tina says. Her eyes soften as they meet his. "When most people look into the abyss of death, they are afraid. Many don't know what they're looking at. But you, you just feel rage. You're angry at the person who took your life, and the disease that took your wife's. And I know that getting into Heaven didn't make that better. It's like your heart is on fire. That won't go away. But if you stay long enough to help us, to help those people, I will take it away."

"Why didn't you just ask me to do this?"

"Free will." Tina slides another piece of paper across the table.

"I just got comfortable," Chris quietly groans. He crawls to the table. The paper is a lavender cardstock. On top is a keycard to the elevator. "What's this?"

"This is your first mentee," Tina says. "His name is Lucas."

"Encephalitis guy. Wait, how did—"

"Right," Tina says. "A familiar face. He'll be finished with orientation in the coming weeks. Check your mailbox for others. They'll be in Ulie's position. Hopeless cases to a degree. Just help them move on. Now, take that, and return to the elevator."

Chris turns his attention from the glowing purple and gold keycard back to Tina. After a blurry moment to glare, he scans the nothingness of the rest of the room. "Do you have another appointment?"

"We have a meeting," Tina says coldly.

"You're going to argue."

"You'll find the elevator behind you. Insert the keycard into the slot, and it'll take you where you need to go."

"Anyone else hungry?" Judith says. "It's almost supper time."

Chris feels something in him pulling toward the elevator. He slides the keycard into the slot and the elevator opens. He steps in and the doors close on the white room. He waits for the elevator to arrive…wherever. He supposes sometimes the waiting isn't always the worst part. Chris falls against the corner of the elevator as it moves toward where he needs to go. He thinks about Andrea. He's okay with not being able to conjure her face. A burp stirs within him. He stifles it. The burning sensation brings up Aditi's face. He remembers her saying that death is just the separation between two lives that have nothing to do with one other. He had tried so hard to hold his life together. A flush of embarrassment reddens his face. A yellow light flashes between the elevator doors. The light reflects off the golden envelope in his hand, and his drunken embarrassment becomes drunken pride in his new friend. As the light flashes faster,

Chris shields his eyes with the description of his first mentee.

The doors open to the Purgatory Enterprises mailroom hallway. The distinct smell of body odor twists his weakened stomach. He dry heaves but manages to keep everything inside. He steps into the bright hallway. He sees Ulie through squinted eyes. The large Russian man is crouching over the combination dial of his mailbox.

"Don't bother," Chris says. He holds out the gold envelop.

Ulie's crooked smile spreads across his face. "Ma," he says, weakly. His hands shake as he reaches for the envelope. He takes it and embraces Chris. The vertebrae in Chris's back crackle. Chris squeezes back.

"You're on the chopping block, bud."

## ABOUT THE AUTHOR

Josh Stricklin is a writer from Mississippi.

...

# So You're Dead

...

Well not to be all Ferris Bueller, but that was it.

If you stop turning pages, there will be no more pages to turn.

Okay...you asked for it. Here's some stories from my college days. Including the inspiration for the final book from Under the Wolf Tree, *There's Something in the Smoke*, coming soon.

# Bonus Content

# What We Do for Love

A child shrieked from a booth of the restaurant area as Derek crossed the lobby of the Big Spender Casino. The sound was a snake's rattle to his ears. He popped another cough drop, feeling as thin and brittle as he looked. Derek finished straightening his bowtie watching the lights from the slot machines chase each other up and down the high walls of the casino. Another shriek. The mother offered the boy more fries and the remainder of the hamburger from his plate. Meaty toddler limbs flailed in the air. Giving up, the mother slid her plate of spaghetti in front of him, and the tantrum quickly tapered away.

*She'll have to send that kid through a carwash,* Derek thought as he continued to the bar. He rolled his sleeves up to the elbow revealing several tattoos on each forearm.

Derek pushed through the waist-high swinging doors to the bar, covering his cough with the crook of his elbow. He couldn't stop himself from grinning when he saw Jackie biting her lip to keep from laughing in the ear of whoever was on the other end of the phone call.

"Well, I've got to go," Jackie said, stifling a laugh. "Not a problem. I'll ask God to send a little help your way. Okay, bye-bye dear." She dropped the phone into her apron pocket and laughed into her hands. "You still ain't coughed that lung out, hun? It's been a month."

"Almost two. I'm going to die with this cough. Who was that?"

"It was Mary," she said. She shook the giggles out of her system.

"What's so funny?"

"Her uncle died."

"That's horrible," Derek said, not without a smile creeping across his face.

"He died in a really funny way."

"*You* are horrible." Derek tossed a towel in her face.

"Thank you for coming in so early," she said more seriously. "Anthony'll be here any minute to drop off the kids. I know you don't like getting involved with my drama."

"The extra time on the clock always helps. Besides you know I don't mind."

"I would. He's obsessed with himself. Talking to him is talking to a teenager who just disagrees to be a bastard. He's basically what would happen if the Internet took human form."

"I don't know why you even let him see your kids after everything he's done."

"Kids need a dad. Even it means having one that shows them how not to act. Of all the people in the world to become Internet famous, it had to be the one I divorced. That's being a mom, I guess. I'd go full-on Barry Bonds on that ridiculous truck, and hoof him in the berries, but I don't want to give the state a reason to get even more involved than it is. At least he's holding up that much of his deal."

"It wouldn't be good for your kids to see you 'hoof him in the berries' anyway."

Jackie watched him tie his apron around his waist. "How did Jean's surgery—" Her attention turned toward low rumble of bass swelling from the parking lot. She could see the black dually truck through glass doors facing the parking lot. The neon *Big Spender Casino* lights reflected off the pristine paint and tinted windows. She correctly assumed he kept it that clean to check mustache and sideburns on the go. "And there's Mr. YouTube now."

"And so, it begins. I'll take care of it," Derek said. "Just the kids or a check too?"

"Both. Please, don't get too close to his mouth. I don't want you to smell hooker and chewing tobacco for the rest of my shift."

"Don't be filthy." Derek walked to the entrance to the casino, using his sleeve to catch his cough. He opened the glass door, and bass flooded the lobby behind a frigid wind. "Hey!" Derek shouted. A plume of fog barreled from his mouth. The rumble of the bass vibrated in his chest.

The back door opened. Two little feet dangled between the bottom of the door and the ground. Mandy, the older of Jackie's two kids, dropped down and sprinted to Derek for a full-force hug. She said something, but there was no chance he would be able to hear what it was. He caught her midstride as Libby's tiny feet came into view below the door.

The feet dangled for a few moments as Derek and Mandy walked together toward the truck. Then, Libby fell onto the asphalt. Tears started immediately. The deafening music continued.

"Hey!" Derek shouted. In one swift motion he scooped Mandy

into his arm and scrambled to Libby. "Libby, are you okay, sweetie?"

Libby continued to cry. Her palms were badly scraped. Derek stood her up and spoke into Mandy's ears, "Can you help your sister get to your mom? Thank you, sweetie."

Derek snapped to an upright position. He slammed the truck's back door. He shouted at the buzzing tented windows and rapped on the window with his fist.

"Hey, hey, hey!" Anthony said. The sight of tobacco grains in Anthony's teeth triggered Derek's gag reflex. "The hell's your problem? You got prints on my—"

"Why don't you make America great again and turn this fucking truck off," Derek shouted. The engine died. "Did you see Libby?"

"Yeah, I seen her. I'm dropping her off. Hold up." He answered his cellphone. "Yo."

Derek quickly administered two wakeup slaps through the window.

"Bro! What the—"

"Shut up, Anthony," Derek snapped. His hand shot up stopping more words from pouring out of Anthony's mouth. "Your daughter fell. She was on the ground. Look, you can treat Jackie whatever way you want. At this point we kind of think it's funny. It gives us something to make fun of you for. The Internet shit? Fine. Whatever, but you cannot be a dummy when your kid is on the ground. Not everything is on the Internet. You have to be in the actual real world."

"Dude, just take the check," Anthony pleaded.

Derek snatched it from his hand. "Life is longer than fifteen minutes. You need to care about something real."

"Fuck you, Derek," Anthony said just before the window was completely rolled up. The truck roared to life, revving obnoxiously. The smell of burnt rubber filled the parking lot as Anthony sped toward the highway and out of Derek's vision.

Derek reentered the Big Spender Casino with the check in his hand. He rolled his shoulders, sloughing away the anger and coughed into his elbow.

"See," Jackie said, drying Libby's palms with a new hand towel. "No big deal. You're tough. Go play with your sister in the back." Jackie handed Libby a keycard. The kids giggled and bounced away. Jackie watched them until they got to the breakroom door. "Was he a pill?"

"Just like always." Derek handed Jackie the check.

"Thank you," Jackie said. She hugged Derek, verifying the check's amount behind his back. "I'm sorry to get you involved."

"You know I don't mind." He pulled a rag out of the sink and wiped down the bar.

Jackie watched for a moment, admiring him. "How'd Jean's surgery go, by the way?"

"She's great," Derek said. "Now that we paid what the insurance wouldn't, I feel like I can afford go to the doctor myself. Which is good, because I could make her worse if I still have a cough while she recovers."

"You're a good dude." Jackie grinned at him. The slot machines, the winners, and the losers filled the silence. "Let me tell you how Mary's uncle died."

"Jesus," Derek laughed.

# The Smoke

*You'll be all right.* That was the last thing Sam told Rebecca as she watched the world change. It snowed that day. That wet snow that doesn't stick. The ground had been wet ever since then.

Rebecca listened and watched the quarter acre of Missouri backwoods around her. Her eyes naturally gravitated back to the splintered rocking chair across from her on the small back porch of the church. It was one of many things that could use a fresh coat of paint, or new parts around here. Her hand rested on its armrest. The memory of Sam sitting in that chair was the residue of marker on a white board. Her fingers picked at the uneven wood where the familiar hand always seemed to be. Sam was gone and so recently that grief still hadn't taken over her.

The smell of smoke brought her back to the quarter-acre of her vision. Beyond that, the trees blurred to vague shapes of gray growing more implied in the smoke that perpetually thickened the air swallowed them.

Her stomach growled. It growled every day. All the time. Her hands rested on her muddy jeans. Her fingers toyed with the frayed denim around her knees. Blood had dried on the sleeve of her blue plaid shirt, turning it a muddy purple. It was Sam's, and that's why she still hadn't washed it. Then something shattered the silence.

*There's something in the smoke,* she thought.

Rebecca swiped the pistol from the seat of Sam's chair. Making her way towards the sound using stones and muddy walkways to mute her footsteps, she checked the clip. She had checked it before, but she had already learned that being in the smoke wasn't the best time to find out you forgot a step. She tightened her ponytail, being mindful of the still tender bruise on the back of her neck and marched toward the woods. She stopped at the shoulder of a muddy dirt road. She listened for the footsteps, looking into the woods for some sign of life, but all she saw were trees and the hazy shapes of more trees. The air smelled like dirty fire. Rebecca steeled herself against the incredible urge to sprint blindly into the woods.

Nothing came to her for so long that she considered whether she really heard—

Something fell. Rebecca heard the rusty deer trap clamp shut followed by a loud shout confirming her fear that she was no longer the only person here. She entered the woods behind the rigidly aimed pistol in her hands. She carefully and quickly made her way toward the sound. She started to give up again, chalking this one, too, up to cabin fever. It had been a long time since she had heard another voice, and even longer since something good came out of the woods. Maybe she was just imagining things.

Then Rebecca saw a dark blue mound materialize out of the smoke. It moved, and when it did, she heard the familiar sound of rustling leaves.

"Don't move," she shouted. That authority she had used before everything changed assembled her words into an unavoidable weapon. The person froze. Rebecca moved in closer. She watched him like he was the only thing in the world, and with the world being limited to the quarter-acre of her vision, he might as well have been.

"You want a smoke?" the man said through a pain-riddled grimace. He was on all fours and his bodied swelled with every heaving breath. His hair and beard were the same white that hers had been before. The wrinkles on his face, however, suggested that his wouldn't fade back to blonde the way hers had already started to do. Mud caked his jeans up to the shins. One thing stood out more than all the rest about him. They were wearing the same blue flannel shirt.

"No, I don't want a smoke," she snapped, nearly confused by the lighthearted tone at the bedrock of his voice. She started to raise the gun but thought of Sam. How would he feel about the way she handled this? Dead leaves crunched as she repositioned her feet. She focused on maintaining the unexcited ebb and flow rhythm of her breathing. If she could control that, she could control the rest of the situation. "What do you want?"

"I'm going to roll onto my butt, Okay? I'll move slow; I just can't stay in this position. My knees ain't what they were. Not like I can go anywhere anyway." He weakly lifted the hand stuck in the deer trap. The chain pulled tight against the stake in the ground. He waited for rejection. "I take it you're fine with that?"

"Go on."

The man rocked from his hands and knees to a seated position.

"You ain't gonna shoot me with that, are ya?" He asked, chuckling. "At least go get something bigger. You sure you don't want a smoke?"

"Yes."

"Mind if I have one?"

"Where did you come from?" Rebecca asked. "The city?"

"What city?" he asked around the cigarette in his mouth.

"St. Louis," she said, exasperated.

"*St. Louis?*" He looked around himself, genuinely stunned. "Well, shit. I'm going the wrong way."

"What are you doing out here?"

"Well, I was looking for my dog, Sadie." He reached into his shirt pocket and retrieved a cracked polaroid of himself and a fattish brown pit bull on a porch swing. They both wore big goofy smiles. "Have you seen her?"

"What's your name?"

"John," he answered, reluctantly switching his tone to fit hers. "What's yours?"

"I haven't seen your dog, John."

"Her name is Sadie."

Rebecca raised the pistol.

"Whoa, what are you doing?" John began pulling at the rusty jaws of the deer trap.

"You'll come back."

"No, really," he said. The deer trap started to budge. "Look, I just want my dog."

"They always come back," she said.

Leaves crunched somewhere in the smoke just beyond Rebecca's vision. She shushed him. She listened to the footfalls. It wasn't a dog. They were spread to two distinct points to her right. She spun toward the sounds, keeping John in her peripheral sight. She refused to let them fully surround her. "Who are you with," she whispered.

"No one," John breathed. "I'm just looking for my dog. Sadie."

She held her hand up, silently shushing him. She peered around the small plot of land that she could see. "There's someone in the smoke."

The footsteps closed in on them, and she could see the dark shapes of people materializing. She trained the pistol on them.

"Well look at this," one of the men said. The voice was a spotlight of unwelcomed familiarity. He was scrawny and wore multiple sweatshirts. His muddy jeans were ripped at both knees. He was balding, and there were scrapes all along his bald spots and down his face. His mouth appeared to be wet like he had been eating something greasy. The wild look in his eyes stirred an uneasiness in Rebecca, and she tightened her grip on the pistol.

"Where's your house, sweetheart?" the other said. The wife-beater under his flannel shirt was ripped across his stomach. His black hair clung to his sweaty face. There were bloodstains around the holes in his clothes. "It's dangerous out here. Shouldn't you be all locked up and safe?"

"She gotta popgun this time," the first one noticed. He wiped at his wet mouth. "See it? Better be careful around this one."

"They always come back," Rebecca said, looking over her shoulder at John.

"Don't come any closer," she told the two men. She gestured toward John. "Do you know this guy?"

"They don't know me," John said.

"Oh yeah," the bald one said. "We know him."

"Who do you think told us how to get here?"

"I don't know them," John said. Rebecca saw out of the corner of his eye that he was now pulling on the stake in the muddy ground with both hands. He'd be free soon and with a weapon.

"What's his name then?" she asked them.

"What do you mean, 'what's his name,'" the second man mocked. "I'm not going to tell you his name. Not when you won't tell us yours."

"They don't know me," John said again. The stake loosened in the soft ground. "I'm just looking for my dog, Sadie."

"Be quiet," she said.

Her vision only briefly shifted from the two men standing between her and the smoke to John. They charged her. The bald man ducked under her aim. He clamped his arms around her and squeezed. Her grip on the pistol weakened. The other man snatched the gun out of her hand and tossed it in the dead leaves. He grabbed her shirt, ripping the highest button from the seam.

"I told you we weren't going to be as nice when we came back."

John hobbled to his feet with the deer trap in his hand. He lunged forward and clipped the bald man in the back of the head. His unconscious body thumped on the ground.

Rebecca sent her foot, toe-up, between the sweaty man's legs. She pushed him to the ground and rushed to where the pistol landed. She dug through the dead leaves, feeling for cold metal. The sweaty man stumbled to his feet and ran back into the smoke swearing at her. He faded out of sight in a matter of steps.

Rebecca released a cry of discovery and whipped around to John. She followed the pistol toward him. She nudged the bald man on the ground with her foot. He didn't move, but she saw the slow rise and fall of his chest from beneath the sweatshirts.

John froze moving only to breathe and raise his hands.

"Get back on your knees," she shouted.

"I'm sorry," John said. "I shouldn't have made light of you finding me. I can't imagine what this has done to you. I'm not here to hurt you. I'm just looking for my dog, Sadie."

"Will you please stop saying her name?"

"How else is she going to hear me calling her, if I don't say her name?"

"You brought them here."

"I didn't." John pleaded. "Please. Just put it down."

"You'll come back."

"I won't."

"They always come back."

"Please. I just want my dog."

Rebecca tightened her grip on the butt of the pistol.

"What's your name," John asked. It was an act of desperation. He was trying to distract her. Make her forget about the world outside this quarter-acre of woods.

She started to say something but instead made the nearly imperceptible motion of putting her finger one the trigger.

John lowered his hands. "Please," he said. "She'll be out there alone."

*He's lying. He'll be right back here just like the others.*

"Just like you."

*They always come back.*

Then, she heard a bark. Her eyes met John's.

"Sadie!" John shouted. The barking continued. It mingled with the sound of crunching leaves.

Rebecca's eyes darted toward the sounds. John called his dog again. Then she saw her. The fattish brown pit bull lumbered out of the smoke and toward John. She tackled him, painting his face with doggie kisses.

The pistol hung in Rebecca hand at her thigh. She stared over him to nothing. She felt hollow. Clean tears stung her eyes.

John climbed to his feet. "Sadie, sit."

Sadie sat.

John stepped toward her, bringing her attention and watery eyes to him.

"Let's put that down," John said. He lifted the gun from her weak fingers and laid it on the ground.

Rebecca fell to a seated position on the ground. John rolled his eyes and eased his bulk down beside her. They sat there together in the woods staring into the smoke. "I'm so tired, John."

Sadie sat next to John. He reached into his shirt pocket. "You want a smoke?"

"My name is Rebecca."

"You want a smoke, Rebecca?" John was finally able to take a deep drag. He held the mostly empty pack of cigarettes up to her.

"I would've shot you," Rebecca said. Her bottom lip trembled.

"You didn't," John said. He returned the lighter and pack to his shirt pocket.

"I'm sorry," she said. Tears fell in her lap.

"No, I am. I have no idea what you've gone through out here. But someone should apologize for it." John watched her fiddling with her buttons. "What are you doing?"

"It's for your hand." Rebecca offered her shirt. Sam's blood stared back at her from the cuff. She looked away from it and down at the brown Pearl Jam shirt she still wore. "It's probably broken, but we can use the sleeve to set it."

"It's not broken." He flexed his purple hand as proof. "Just gonna hurt a while."

"You want some water?"

"She'll take some if you have anything clean." John pulled Sadie to him, petting her soft chest.

"There's water at the church. It's clean."

She thought of Sam's words as she felt the world change again. *You'll be all right.*

# Mississippy River

I knew her well, Miss Brimley. She gave me money to cut this grass even though I told her I would do it for free.

Please sit, Miss Brimley. I know we on a lonely road, but if someone does drive by, I don't want to let them think I made you stand.

Thank you.

No, I ain't about to ask you to reconsider. A highway's gone be here whether or not I like it. Least I can do is tell you where the bodies are buried if you gone go digging in the yard.

Tea? Don't worry. It ain't poisoned. It's sweet. See? You won, Miss Brimley. You just here so I can tell you why we been fighting in the first place. I know it was a pain dealing with me for the longest time, but that's just how people in a small town are. You rile us up, and we'll go like a hot damn. Doesn't matter if we're right or not. You got no idea how many people are buried in the dirt they fought over. Please, Miss Brimley. Just have a glass.

Thank you.

Look, you ain't from here. Maybe you run this county now, but you hadn't been here long enough to know the story. Maybe you heard some, but if you won't budge—or if you can't as you say—you need to understand why she meant something special to this part of town—why I been cutting this grass the past couple years even though she's gone.

Her name was Madeline Rosenburg. A lot of folks called her Maddie or Rose. I only ever called her Miss Maddie though. Didn't feel right calling an adult by her first name.

She was born here. Not many people could say that back then. Her momma brung Miss Maddie here in her belly from Hawaii. They moved here in this house, and when I tell you she was born here, this house is what I mean. It was a lot more common in the 20s. They didn't have hospitals for poor people back then. Not even the one on the back way out of town. That one that looks more like a prison than hospital.

But anyway.

Her family was farmers. Here and back on the islands. That's why they got so much land behind that house. That's America, right? Bring us your tired, your poor, your huddled masses yearning to breathe free, and let them strike it rich and what not. I don't know why they'd come to Rose Colline, Louisiana of all places, but they did. Not that I got it all together my-damn-self. I live here too after all.

Whatever the reason, they plopped down right here and made a farm. Her daddy dug that field hisself. One row at a time—little by little—this all became a sugar farm. They struggled like everybody else. You know they weren't the only one in the area. The Thibodauxs still got the sugar farm on the other side of the Baton Rouge—and they still do okay after their owner came up missing a few years back—and there's another one up near Slidell. Not sure who has that one. Lot of sugar in one place. They were on top of each other like coats of paint, but once that second great war got going real good, business got busy. Miss Maddie did her part too. She was a little toddler carrying around a pail and wetting the ground after her momma and became a teenager taking the horses up the road to the store for tools. She grew up fast on that farm, and unlike most people from Rose Colline, found herself unmarried at twenty years old.

This town? Twenty? In the 1940s? She was a witch. Not really, but you know.

Miss Brimley, I seen the pictures. I seen her on her deathbed. She didn't look a blink over forty, and that was in '82. What I mean by that is she was younger than her age, and when Adam Broussard came into Turner's Building Supply, he looked nearly twice her age rather than just three years her elder. Her black hair and dark skin may as well have been a spotlight. She wasn't small neither. Five-ten. Five-eleven. I'm six-two, and she never had a problem looking me in the eye. She was thin but not frail. The muscles in her arms swelled with natural strength.

This was '46 some time and things were getting back to normal again. When Adam Broussard first saw her though the shelving, she was carrying a thirty-five-pound sack of feed with no sign of any real effort. My dad told me that.

That's right Benjamin Turner was my dad. I'm Matthew Turner. Owner of Turner Building Supply for twenty-five years now. I told you I didn't need her money. And I don't need yours. It's the principle. In both cases.

The moment right before Adam put his eyes on Miss Maddie as

she was going through the shelves for a spade was the last moment Miss Maddie wasn't somewhere in his thoughts. That's what she told me anyway. There are people who come into your life Miss Brimley—and maybe this has happened to you—but you find yourself doing things for them. Things you don't do for other people. It's not that you do despite not wanting to, because you do. You almost *have* to do something for them—something like carry a thirty-five-pound bag of horse feed around a hardware store—just to be in that person's life. And that's what Miss Maddie what for Adam Broussard.

He was even taller than her, and he looked like a dirty mop with his long, wet hair combed to a point in the back like a duck's ass. He moved his gangly frame in her direction. He had all the grace of a man who had spent an hour in a tumble dryer. Somehow, he composed hisself enough to approach her without running her off.

"Hi," Adam said. He wiped his forehead with a handkerchief.

"Hello," Miss Maddie answered. She added a smile for courtesy's sake and continued through the shelves.

"I like your hair," he said. He shifted his weight from one foot to the other. "Most ladies wear their hair down."

"It gets in my face when I work."

"I like it."

Miss Maddie turned to him. She watched him for a moment, confused. "Thanks."

"Here," Adam said. He reached for the bag.

"What are you doing?" She pulled the bag away from him.

"I just want to help."

"It's fine. I've got it."

"Wouldn't it be easier to look for little shovels with both your hands free?" He waited.

She watched him again but relented.

Adam took the sack, hefting it onto his shoulders.

"Thank you," she said again. She was cautious of him, but he was right. Finding the right size spade was easier with free hands. She plucked on off the shelf, examined it, and turned to Adam. "This is what I needed," she said. "I can take it back now."

"No, no," Adam said. The strain in his face brought up fresh veins in his neck. "I can just carry it to the counter for you. No be deal."

"You're sure about that?"

"Yes, ma'am," Adam said. "It's not a problem. What's your name, Mrs...?"

"Miss Rosenberg. Madeline, but Maddie is fine."

Adam shifted the feed on his shoulder and offered his hand. "I'm Adam. Broussard."

"Why do I know that name?" Miss Maddie started toward the front counter, walking very slowly. She always said it was because she wanted to see if the sack of feed would fold Adam in half or break him. I believe differently.

"I'm the mayor."

"I've lived here all my life; how have I never met you before?"

"I'm from Kenner. I wanted to start a career. The seat for mayor was available, so I applied for office?"

"Applied? I thought you had to be elected."

"Yes, ma'am. If someone is impeached because of a murder and a subsequent cover up, everyone gets booted. After a week, the seat becomes available to anyone if no one in town wants to run."

"So, you applied?"

"I applied."

"But you're only a year or two older than me."

"I'm twenty-three. That's old enough."

"Still. It's a big job for someone who's never held office of any kind."

"It's a small town."

"That's exactly my point."

"Well, this is my promise," Adam dropped the bag of fee on the counter and shook the strain from his shoulder out through his fingertips. "If your life isn't better in a year, I'll step down. Deal?"

Miss Maddie put the spade on the counter, taking one final look up and down Adam. "Deal. I'm holding you to that."

"I expect it."

"How are we today, Miss Rose?" my dad said.

"Good and you, Mr. Benji?"

"Benji," my dad said. He always said that. "Oh, not so bad."

"I met the mayor today," Miss Maddie said.

"Oh, did ya now?"

"He was okay."

Adam chuckled nervously.

"Well, that's just fine. How's your pop?" dad asked.

"He's still in bed. I was going to ask if you could send one of the boys to come get the tall grass."

"Oh, no, Miss Rose. I just sent the twins to their grandmother's in New Orleans."

"Oh, that's find. I'll get to it in the morning. I'll just have to get up early."

"I can send Matthew," dad joked. "He's walking now and pert near ready to work."

Miss Maddie laughed. Probably too hard, as she was apt to do. "That's okay, Benji." She turned back to Adam. "Thank you for carrying my bag."

"It's not problem," Adam said with extra enthusiasm. "I don't mind helping you get it home."

"That's not necessary," she answered. "It's a bit of a ride on the horse, but I'll be fine." Miss Maddie smiled at him, left her dollars on the counter, and left the store. Adam watched her do it all.

"You better close your mouth, bud," my dad said. "Bugs will fly in there."

"Do you think she—"

"I don't. You got a lot to work on."

"What do you mean?"

"Well, for one, you wear that white suit as a sign of power," dad said. "But all she sees, is a man with soft hands and clean clothes. That's a woman who knows how to work. She'll want a man that does, too."

Adam stood there, watching the open space where Miss Maddie had been standing.

Outside the store, Miss Maddie crossed the dirt road to her horse. That was the first time she saw the man in the black suit. I mean black. Shoes with black buckles, pants, shirt, *and* jacket. He even had a black hat like that one coach from Alabama. I forget what it's called, only this man's was all black, not checkered. I know it's harmless thinking of a man in a suit, like Johnny Cash, but there's something unsettling about seeing it. It was too pure. Too clean. Every road in Rose Colline is dirt, and when I seen that man in the black suit, we were paving them all. Dirt was always in the air. But that suit never had a speck of dirt on it. I doubt it even does now.

But anyway.

Miss Maddie got home just before lunch. Her daddy had moved to the front porch. I think he had the flu. He was pale and wrapped in a ton of blankets. When she saw him, he was staring off into the sky like he was unplugged.

"Daddy, what are you doing?"

Her mom popped up from the garden. "He wanted to come outside. Wouldn't hush up about it. I told him he was just going to make it worse."

"Okay, you've gotten your fresh air, now back inside." Her daddy groaned as she helped him to his feet. "Come on. Let's get some food and get back in back."

Her mother helped with lunch, and by the afternoon, her daddy was back in bed.

Miss Maddie went outside to feed the horses when she noticed the flap on the mailbox dangling. They never received mail, and she didn't know what to make of it at first. She quickly walked to the mailbox, and waiting for her was a piece of paper folded in half. No stamp. No envelope. She opened the paper. Someone had taken the time to type the message. It read:

"The war is over. Close up shop before you start another one."

She heard an engine then. Behind her, an old truck rumbled down the dirt road in her direction. She jammed the paper into her pants pocket and waited for the truck to stop. She didn't recognize the truck, but the face behind the wheel would've stood out in a crowd of millions. Adam flashed a smile her way, but it wasn't until he pulled the reel lawn mower—one of those that ain't got an engine in it—out of the back of that truck that she understood why he was there. A rush of embarrassment reddened her face.

"What are you doing?" Miss Maddie asked, bewildered.

"I heard you needed help with your grass."

"And you're going to cut it with that little thing?"

"Why not? It's my personal mower. Works fine on my yard."

"Sure," Miss Maddie said, sweeping her arm across the yard. "But all this?"

Adam swallowed hard. "Grass is grass," he said weakly. "And I need your vote."

"Well, have fun, Mr. Mayor." Miss Maddie clapped him on the shoulder.

She kept a curious eye on his progress as she started, continued, and finished with her chores. When the sun burned the horizon, Miss Maddie brought Adam a glass of tea. "You're going good work out here."

Adam took the tea and downed it in one go. His white shirt was soaked all the way through. It clung to him like a thick film over his torso. Even his pants were soaked to the knees with sweat. He heaved breath. "Thanks. That was delicious."

"Did you even taste it?" She smiled, admiring him in that moment.

He laughed. "It's getting dark. I'm going to have to come back when I can see."

"You don't have to do that. I can finish."

"No, no," he said. "I said I'd cut your grass. I can't leave a job undone."

She looked up at him. Her grinned widened. "You'll come back here in the morning?"

"I'll have to be here before the sun gets too far up. I'm helping a school get its doors open before the school year."

"My mom says you're sweet on me."

He gaped at her. "I…"

"It's nice," she said. "Be here in the morning, and I'll fix you some breakfast. You can use the tractor. It'll take about an hour to finish."

"There's a tractor?"

"And if you need help with the school, I'll come with you."

"You will?"

"I can't go to the grave owing you a favor." Miss Maddie squeezed his arm. Her fingers came away wet. "Thank you." She walked back to the house.

"I'll see you in the morning," he called back. He tossed the lawnmower into the bed of the truck. He tried to hide his smile, but Miss Maddie could see it through the kitchen window. I imagine he didn't sleep for hours when he got home. I know I didn't when that feeling overcame me. Regardless, he was there again with the roosters the next morning.

It only took Adam about ten minutes to figure out how to work the tractor and another twenty to get the blades attached to the back of it. As promised, he finished the grass and in less time that she figured. Miss Maddie was waiting on the porch with some eggs and bacon when he finished. He thanked her and ate quickly.

"What do you have to do for the school?" Miss Maddie asked.

Adam swallowed and wiped his mouth clean. "It's just some administrative meetings. Setting up the chain of command an all those types of things."

"I don't see how I would be any help with that."

"Well, a lot of the teachers have children with no one to watch them. If you can keep an eye on them, that be a huge help."

"I've never watched kids. It's just me and my parents here, I only ever talk to adults. I don't think I can do baby talk."

"Then don't," Adam said. "Just talk to them like they're adults. Who knows. Maybe that's the secret."

Miss Maddie chuckled. "What's the worst that could happen, right?"

And that's what she did. She rode, nervous as all get out, in the dirty truck up to the school. There wasn't a lot to say. Trucks back then were the noisiest things. Adam gave her a brief tour of the school and showed her to the room where the children would be. There were about six or seven kids and there, and yours truly was one of'm. My momma was a music teacher, so that was the first time I ever seen Miss Maddie, but of course I don't remember it that much. Just a flash that I may have put in my memory later in life. She was always kind of there in my life, I can't remember or even imagine a time that she was absent in my life for more than a few months. Certainly not after I started cutting this grass out here. You know, I do remember never being talked to like a baby. No one else ever did that back then. It always felt like you were talking to an adult like an adult.

When Adam came back into the room at the end of the day, Miss Maddie was telling stories like she did. Stories of Hawaiian royalty. We were amazed. Always amazed. There was a tiny group of islands in the middle of the ocean, where there was an entire civilization around volcanos and mountains. I remember one time she told us about a surfer who lived in a hut on the beach. Never even wore shoes. He woke up and surfed and ate fish and slept. He became a spirit of the ocean. That was the life for me. She would've kept going forever, I think, with Adam watching her telling us stories, but our parents came in a collected us.

"You know you're good at this." Adam ushered her into the hall and toward the old truck.

"It's just like you said," Miss Maddie said, grinning. "Just talk to them like their adults. That wasn't so bad."

"You know," Adam began. "You could do this."

"No, I can't. I have the farm."

"You could be a kindergarten teacher though," he said. "You only need to come once a week. Tell your stories. Surely, you won't want to keep up the farm yourself forever."

I think that's when Miss Maddie remembered that note from the mailbox.

"Yeah," she admitted. "Probably not."

The ride back to the farm was much less nervous one. She even felt more comfortable around him. As the truck rumbled to a stop at the end of the driveway, she asked him, "Do you have time to take a walk before you go?"

"Sure," he said.

"I want to show you something."

Miss Brimley, do you see those woods over there to your right? Just beyond the big tree next to the smaller one. Yeah, right over there. That was her favorite place. Up till that morning she stared death in the face, she went there. It's quiet. There's a tiny stream there. There's a narrow trail between the weak trees—a lot of them are even dead for the most part. When she was a child, she made a little sign out of wood and blue paint that read "Mississippy River" on it, just like a kid would spell if you told them to sound it out. With a "Y" at the end. Her daddy hammered it into the ground hisself.

I took that sign in '82. Put it in my own quiet spot.

She took Adam out to that stream in the woods for the first time that day. Before either of them said anything, they just sat, listening to the water, and wind, and nature. The clean air filled them. Calmed them like it does. A breeze cooled their faces.

"I have to tell you something," Miss Maddie said. She handed Adam the piece of paper from the mailbox. "Someone is threatening us, and I don't know what to do about it."

"Who do this?" Adam said, grimacing at the paper.

"I don't know," she answered. "There's no other sugarcane farm in town, and we mind our business. I found that in the mailbox before you showed up for the grass. I'm glad you did show up, because I would'a went straight to momma with this. I think that would have her wound like guitar string. I thought it'd be best to show you first."

"I'll give this to sheriff Maxie and see what he says."

"Thank you." Miss Maddie kissed his cheek. She left her head on his shoulder.

"I don't think Mississippi has a 'Y' at the end of it."

"I was a kid when I made that sign. I thought this was the Mississippi. My daddy hammered it up for me."

"He didn't correct the spelling for you?"

"Well, I know how to spell it now. Besides, didn't your dad ever let you believe in something silly just because you were a kid? Like the Santa Claus or something?"

"I never met my dad," Adam said. "And my mom was dying for most of my childhood."

"Oh," Miss Maddie said. "I'm so sorry."

"No, no. I'm doing just fine. I'd even argue that I'd have been able to come here and be mayor if my life had been any different. Not that I'm thankful, but this way we did meet."

The moment breathed with the flow of water and air around them.

"You say I only need to come one day a week?"

Adam brightened. "Just one. More if you start to like it."

"I can pick the day?"

"Any day you want."

Miss Maddie watched the light reflect off the stream and dance on the tree trunks. She played with the grass around her. "Well, I go into town on Wednesdays for delivery. I'm done by nine. It's kind of a waste to go all the way there for only a few hours."

"You'll have a room ready by next Wednesday."

"Maybe you'll give me a ride in your truck? You can fit a lot more in the back of that thing than in my carriage."

"I'm sure you're right on that account."

"How many times do I gotta smile at you before you kiss me?"

"I guess one."

She smiled at him.

You know, Miss Brimley. Those two got together did a lot of good for a lot of people. Including me. She was my teacher from grade school all the way up. We fought, sure. I mean, she *was* my teacher from grade school all the way up. After we gave my momma back to the lord when she had my sister, Miss Maddie filled a hole in my life. That's something I didn't truly know until '82. I wasn't her only kid neither. Everyone in this town was. We all loved her. She never paid for flowers, but she always had them. When I took over the store, I made sure she had everything she needed for everything she wanted to do.

All that over some grass. I always said that if it was that important to him after a single conversation in a building supply store, the least I could do after everything she did for me was keep it short. Snakes will sneak up on you in tall grass. After everything she'd been through, I was going to be damned if she was going to be taken down by a snake. So, I kept it up for her.

Why didn't he cut it? I'm almost glad you asked.

You remember that note? The one telling Miss Maddie and her parents to close up shop? Well there are a couple downsides to living in a small town. Technology doesn't evolve fast enough. There's never enough money for improvement. Most importantly, policework doesn't get done fast enough. Emergencies happen. Fights break out. Hell, crime happens. Things like that distract because they're louder. More important than threats. More people working emergencies means less people working the non-emergencies. In Rose Colline in the forties, it didn't take much to distract everybody. I don't blame sheriff Maxie, even if he blames hisself. Everything seemed so happy between Miss Maddie and Adam. They was always together, and it had only been a month or two. She was working three days a week, and the school wanted more out of her. Needed it really but *wanted* it from her. As often as the town witnessed those two, walking hand in hand through the street, everyone already had them married in their minds. They kind of forgot about the piece of paper. Everyone but the man in the black suit. He popped up around town, keeping his eyes on the sugar shelves in the grocery stores, no doubt.

Miss Maddie told me that Adam proposed the week this all happened. That's how it happened back then. As a window closes, time speeds up. Her daddy was on his feet by then. Farming in the wintertime isn't exactly strenuous work, so he gave her the week to be with Adam. And of all places she could've gone that first day, so went to the Mississippy River. She lay in his arms on the bank of the stream, looking up through the leaves. She saw the smoke before she smelled it. And she heard it last—that whooshing, popping noise that means life is being devoured. Clouds of smoke barreled across her vision. She thought, *Those clouds are moving so fast.* And that was all the time she had before the head surrounded them. Miss Maddie and Adam shot to their feet. The flames rolled toward them, eating everything. A glass bottle smashed against a weak tree. It irrupted in flames. Someone yelled from the other side of death.

The voice was muffled, but she caught a few words. "Get it all!" Then, "Make sure it won't grow back."

Two more glass bottles broke, and one more landed in the dead leaves, spilling fire onto the ground. They shouted after whoever had thrown the bottles.

"Go, go, go!" The voice shouted.

Miss Maddie caught a glimpse of the man in the black suit, sauntering backward toward the road. He lit a cigarette on another one of those flaming bottles and let it fly. Miss Maddie made to run, but the bottle shattered on a branch and rained fire down at her.

"No!" Adam caught her and pulled her away.

The flames dropped on her dress, and Adam scrambled to put it out. He snatched handfuls of mud from the bottom of the stream and raced to where she had fallen on the ground. She swiped at the flames, and Adam smeared the mud on her dress, killing the fire. He went back to the stream, leaving her on the ground. I still thank God he did that. He dug into the stream with both hands. He stood upright, and the tree cracked. He took a step toward Miss Maddie, and the tree fell.

Miss Maddie shrieked. The tree pinned him to the bottom of the stream. Miss Maddie leapt to her feet. Crying she sprinted into the water. She dug through the water and found his hand. She felt the strength in his arms. She pulled, and that strength weakened. Something opened up, and the water around her turned red. A little at first, then it surrounded her. She lifted the branches, frantically tugging on them. The tree didn't budge. Adam's hand felt for her. HE tugged weakly at her dress. She stopped looking down through tears at his muddy hands. The hand reached for hers. Their fingers laced. She knelt with tears spilling on her cheeks.

"No," she whispered. The power in her body faded. "Please."

She wrapped her hands around his and held them to her chest. She brought him to her lips. She put his hand on her chest. She felt his life leave him. It filled the Mississippy River and flowed around her. Just like the surfer from the stories she used to tell.

Miss Maddie wept.

The fire took more trees, but none fell close enough to take Miss Maddie too.

She was still kneeling in the water when the sheriff showed up. When they pulled that tree up, Adam came with it. He had been impaled, and pinned to the muddy bottom. He had dirty hands. Miss Maddie always reiterated that, and I think she would've wanted me to do that too.

There was a tradition in her family. Instead of a tombstone, they plant trees over the body. Life gives life. Can you find his tree, Miss Brimley?

The man in the black suit, he killed Adam over some sugar, leaving the babies in Miss Maddie's belly without a daddy. Only one of them left the hospital with her momma. That man in the black suit, he took their livelihood. Took a husband. A daddy. For what? Some green paper and some nickels? That don't last. It's memory—the stories—that's what lasts. The world moves on. It forgets. It's up to us to remember the important things. I hope you'll leave those trees—that big one and the smaller one beside it out there—standing where they are when you start building your highway. Not for me. But people underneath them. Miss Maddie brought her stories here from a little island in the middle of the ocean. She told her students those stories, and we told them to our kids. We added hers to them.

But anyway.

For years that man in the black suit came back. Once a year, I guess to make sure his business in Rose Colline was secure. One day I just saw red. I don't know why, but I ran after than man's black car. I didn't know what I was going to do when I got there, but even when he was out of sight I didn't stop running.

"Some people are just no good," she told me. "He'll just keep coming, even after I'm gone. Don't you worry about him."

And when she was gone he still came. But only once. I don't know why I did what I did. I guess I had to prove a ghost wrong. I hope you'll leave those trees where they are. You know what they say. The best place to hide a body is underneath another body.

Okay, that's it. Shut this thing and go watch Ted Lasso or something.

Made in United States
Orlando, FL
09 June 2023

33944724R00082